Helping Children
Cope with
Stress

Helping Children Cope with Stress

Avis Brenner

LexingtonBooks
D.C. Heath and Company
Lexington, Massachusetts
Toronto

Library of Congress Cataloging in Publication Data

Brenner, Avis.
   Helping children cope with stress.

   Includes index.
   1. Stress in children.   2. Stress in children—Etiology.   I. Title.

BF723.S75B74   1984   155.4   83–47502
ISBN 0–669–06678–8 (alk. paper)
ISBN 0–669–08995–8 (pbk.)

Copyright © 1984 by D.C. Heath and Company

Fifth printing, September 1985

Published simultaneously in Canada

Printed in the United States of America on acid-free paper

International Standard Book Number: 0–669–06678–8 Casebound
International Standard Book Number: 0–669–08995–8 Paperbound

Library of Congress Catalog Card Number: 83–47502

To Mannie

Contents

Contents

List of Tables

Preface

She came into my second grade classroom that afternoon and sat and watched Adam, who was always contained and well-behaved. She ignored the rowdy child for whom I had begged her help. "Look out for Adam," she said as she left, "he's about to explode." Twenty minutes later, when the children were quietly gathered around me listening to a story, Adam emptied the pencil sharpener over my head and ran screaming into the hall.

We talked about Adam late that evening and I asked Asya Kadis how she had known he was holding in so much anger. That was the beginning of my training in learning to see the many ways in which children's bodies and actions express their inner feelings. I became adept at listening to meanings when youngsters talked, but often their shoulders, hands, legs, and faces told me far more than their words.

During the twenty years that followed, I moved from school to college teaching but continued to observe children. I sat in hundreds of nurseries, school rooms, and day care centers and watched them at work and play. Each year, my dismay grew as I identified fewer relaxed, happy youngsters and more stressed girls and boys. Inquiry into the backgrounds of the tense children uncovered life situations unlike any I had imagined. It was time for me to educate myself about the reality of being a child in the last quarter of the twentieth century.

With the encouragement of George Miller and the faculty of Lesley College, I established a program to train human service workers to help children cope with stress. Together, the students and I learned from harried professionals dealing with children and families in real-life settings. Researchers came to the campus to share their findings. We read excellent books about specific problems. We heard speakers advocate conflicting causal theories and therapeutic approaches. Each was an expert in one field, but the students needed broader information as they tried to help children who lived in all kinds of dysfunctional home situations. What was required was a synthesis that would describe and evaluate a range of stresses and coping strategies. Practitioners who supervised the Lesley College students' field work reported a similar need.

In response, this book slowly took shape. It describes a spectrum of stresses affecting children from infancy to age twelve and identifies typical coping patterns. It presents many points of view, relying on the reader to choose ways of helping which are congruent with children's abilities and living arrangements. It is designed to be used by people who work with stressed youngsters on a daily basis, that is, teachers, counselors, social workers, mental health personnel, child care staffs, and parents. There is some necessary repetition from one chapter to another to assist readers who use only those sections which apply to the specific issues which interest them.

This book also suggests areas for future investigation. The field of childhood stress is a new one and research is urgently needed. Although some of the described helping techniques have been in use for ten or more years, few have been objectively evaluated. Most theories which form the basis for current intervention strategies are yet to be tested thoroughly. Each chapter indicates areas in which further study is vital.

A further aim is to encourage adults to offer more support to children. It is clear that youngsters can be helped to flourish despite negative experiences in their formative years. Cycles of mistreatment can be broken before puberty. Youngsters need not grow up to repeat the mistakes of their parents. Their natural resilience makes it possible for them to overcome the effects of shattering events if they have help from concerned adults.

This point is dramatically illustrated in the study by Moskovitz (1983) of the adult lives of twenty-four child survivors of the Nazi Holocaust. Her subjects ranged in age from three to eleven at the time that they were brought from the Terezin and Auschwitz concentration camps to live in a group home in England. During the last years of World War II they had witnessed and been subjected to incredible horror. In England, Alice Goldberger and her staff worked to help each child develop self-confidence and a sense of worth. Slowly all were brought to the realization that they could count on adults to be there when needed and to give pleasure as well as fill material needs. The children were taught to be responsible for one another and to live together harmoniously. Some of the youngsters were eventually adopted; others remained in the group home until they could support themselves. With the exception of one woman who became psychotic, all grew up to be compassionate adults. Those who now have children are nurturant parents. According to Moskovitz, "we learn powerfully from these lives that lifelong emotional disability does not automatically follow early trauma, even such devastating, pervasive trauma as experienced here. Apparently, what happens later matters enormously" (Moskovitz 1983, 237).

Mental health seems to be most consistently achieved when children have lasting, emotionally close relationships with one or more caring adults before childhood's end. When parents are unable to supply this need, I believe that other adults must fill the gap. At present, few are doing so. Childhood is undervalued in our self-centered culture. Budgets for children's services are the first to be cut when governments reduce expenditures. Few adults take the time to get to know the youngsters who live in their own neighborhoods; to talk with them and know their joys and fears; or to offer advice, direction, and comfort.

When my mother came to the United States as a lonely, bewildered immigrant, Miss Mahler, her elementary school teacher, devoted her weekends to helping the child learn English, taking her to the library and to museums. She introduced Rose to the members of a local girls' club who became her friends for life. Today, teachers and other helping professionals are taught to avoid personal relationships with the children in their charge. They are admonished to be professional, distant, and protective of their privacy and leisure. I believe that we must reevaluate this stance.

Too many stressed youngsters no longer believe in their own worth or that of others. Violence and pain are accepted as everyday occurrences. If their perceptions remain unchanged, they will grow up to distort their children's lives. Ultimately, our survival as a nation may depend on our ability as a society to provide children with sufficient adult support to enable them to become caring, peaceable citizens.

Reference

Moskovitz, S. 1983. *Love despite hate: Child survivors of the Holocaust and their adult lives.* New York: Schocken Books.

1

Stress and Coping in Childhood

Children's lives have always been stressful. From birth to puberty youngsters face and somehow cope with a myriad of tensions. However in the past twelve years, the number and severity of childhood stresses has increased dramatically. People who work with children report an uneasy sense that youngsters today have fewer sources of adult support, affirmation, and love than in the recent past. In fact, the number of children living in single-parent homes has doubled. There has been a fourfold increase in the number of youngsters living with mothers who have never been married (Bureau of the Census 1982).

We have become aware that children are being pressured to grow up faster and that protected, sheltered young people are a rarity instead of the norm. The statistics suggest some of the reasons for this erosion of childhood. There are literally fewer caring adults living with children. Child abuse, in all forms, is still increasing.

At the same time, a growing number of organizations have dedicated themselves to helping children. Social scientists are studying the phenomenon of childhood stress. This book attempts to synthesize the work being done on behalf of children from birth to twelve years of age. Its aim is to make available to teachers, social workers, mental health personnel, child care staffs, and parents a summary of what is known about each kind of stress and what can be done to help children to cope.

The Nature of Stress

Stress is a part of life. All kinds of events, from the euphoria of falling in love to the stabbing pain of a cut finger, evoke a similar biological response which is called stress (Selye 1974). To date, research on childhood tension has been limited to negative experiences. We do not know as yet the nature of the stress that occurs when a child is chosen captain of the best team, visits a beloved grandparent, or opens a gift and sees a coveted toy. Lists of childhood stresses have been developed which rank life events in order of the amount of tension which adults suppose each will cause for youngsters (Chandler 1982). In these lists, positive experiences such as an outstanding personal achievement or decrease in the number of arguments between parents are uniformly considered by adults to involve low levels of stress for

1

children (Coddington 1972; Cohen-Sandler, Berman, and King 1982). There are no assessments of the degree to which children agree with these adult estimates.

A Spectrum of Childhood Stressors

The volume and quality of research on negative childhood stress make it possible to describe a spectrum of life experiences which range from ordinary to severe in terms of stress. At the ordinary end are events which occur to most children in our society and for which there are fairly well-defined good coping patterns. For example, most parents are aware that older children are likely to be jealous of newborn siblings. They know how youngsters usually act out their jealousy and how they can be helped to cope.

A short distance along from the ordinary end of the spectrum are the stresses which occur when children have only one parent in the home or when they live in multiple-parent, multiple-dwelling households. In these cases, society, particularly through television, is beginning to outline a variety of ways in which youngsters can cope and thrive. Teachers faced with more and more children in such living situations have helped them to define their problems and seek constructive solutions.

Toward the severe end of the spectrum is the stress caused by separation of children from their parents or siblings. Healthy coping strategies are less well-delineated and society has been less able to spell out its attitudes towards this group of lonely youngsters. Some are well cared for and others are ignored when there is a separation caused by divorce, death, illness, incarceration, or foster placement.

At the severe extreme of the spectrum are those stressors which occur to relatively few children but which are so long-lasting as to require the child to make major personality adaptations in order to survive. Victims of incest, for instance, have no coping guidelines prepared for them by society. Through fear and shame, they remain unknown to their teachers and relatives and receive little support.

Also at the severe end of the spectrum are the children who live for years in situations of abuse, neglect, and parental alcoholism. Society's attitude is one of horror at the situation and blame for the parents. There is considerable public outcry for court intervention and punishment of the adults, ignoring the fact that these corrective actions cause additional stress for children.

Combinations of Stresses

Usually more than one stress occurs at a time in a child's life. Recent research suggests that when several stresses are combined, the effects are more likely to increase geometrically than to be simply additive. In a carefully designed study, Rutter (1979) showed that ten-year-olds living in London under two chronic life stresses were four times as likely to eventually need psychiatric care as youngsters who had to cope with only one chronic stress. He found a similar multiplier effect for children who were exposed to more than one short-term strain at a time. In fact, these brief tensions, which Lazarus calls *hassles*, also exhibit a multiplier effect. In adults, Lazarus and his colleagues found that numerous concurrent hassles have deeper effects on mental health than individual instances of major stress (Kanner, Coyne, Schaeffer, and Lazarus 1981).

Ecology of Stress

The sources of tension for children can be understood by employing the concept of interaction among the ecological factors in their lives. Belsky (1980) and Bronfenbrenner (1979) postulate that youngsters live simultaneously in a microsystem, an exosystem, and a macrosystem. If these systems are visualized as concentric circles, the microsystem is in the center completely surrounded by the exosystem. In its turn, the exosystem is enclosed within the macrosystem. By examining the stressors in each system and recognizing that each continuously interacts with and affects the others, it becomes possible to appreciate the complexity of childhood stress.

The microsystem consists of the child's own characteristics, his family setting, and interaction patterns. Stress in the microsystem can be caused by the process of maturing physically, intellectually, and emotionally; becoming the object of new rules and regulations; and being required to take responsibility for self and siblings. Changes in the microsystem produce stress as the family adds new members and adjusts to the varying needs of children and adults.

The exosystem encompasses the family's social networks of acquaintances, friends, and relatives. It includes the neighborhood in which they live and the children's school and day care arrangements. Exosystem sources of stress arise when families move to new homes, add or subtract relatives, join or leave religious organizations, and when there are changes in parental employment status.

Encircling both the micro- and exosystems, the macrosystem is made up of those cultural values and beliefs evident in the surrounding larger society. Stress occurs when a family deviates from accepted cultural norms.

A child's first day of school is an example of the way in which the three systems interact. Long before the day, factors in the macrosystem (i.e., society's attitudes toward education) begin their impact on children. Television and newspapers show youngsters hating to enter the classroom. Clearly, society expects them to be under stress each year on the first day of school. Influenced by macrosystem pressures, friends and neighbors commiserate with children for having to return to school. Classmates conjure up horror stories about the terrible teacher they will have this year. Under exosystem influences, microsystem stresses mount. Children who dislike school have their distress heightened. Those who love it are dismayed at how different they are from everybody else.

Coping with Stress

As stress is a part of life, so too is the act of coping with unexpected events and adapting to long-term changes. Coping always involves mental and/or physical action. Over time, patterns of coping are developed for specific stressors. These become habitual or routine and are termed adaptations (Iscoe 1977).

Babies begin to cope as soon as they are born. Murphy and Moriarty's (1976) longitudinal study of middle-class children in Topeka, Kansas, found that as early as four weeks after birth, infants have habitual ways of responding to new experiences. The patterns they establish as infants are modified but not basically changed as they grow to be toddlers and preschoolers. The baby who looks long and hard at a new toy before reaching for it is also the toddler who stands in the nursery school doorway and watches the other children before joining their play.

While maintaining innate patterns, youngsters learn additional coping modes from parents, peers, teachers, and relatives. Because their abilities develop over time, it is tempting to make lists of coping techniques which are typical of children at different stages in their growth. Certainly, three-year-olds are more apt to cope with loneliness by inventing imaginary friends than are eleven-year-olds. Yet, we see all kinds of coping mechanisms used quite effectively at every age from birth to puberty.

If we cannot set up an age-stage list of healthy ways of coping, how can we judge the effectiveness of a child's adaptation to stress? The answer to this question is complex. First of all, children seldom use only one strategy at a time. In the course of a day, most respond in several different ways to the same event. For example, when Brian's kitten died, he prepared a shoebox coffin and ceremonially buried it in the backyard. A favorite TV show took his mind off his loss for a while. He spoke sadly of the kitten at supper, was distracted by a game of cards with his older brother, then returned to his grieving again at bedtime, crying himself to sleep. He used three different methods of coping with his stress. It is important, then, to know all of a child's strategies, to examine and weigh them as a group, taking into account how one mode affects the others and how it alleviates or adds to his burden of tension.

Most of the time children are not conscious of their own coping strategies. They simply act without thinking when they are under stress. For example, when his brother went away to college, Kevin responded by spending hours perfecting tiny details on his model airplanes. The concentration made him feel better but he was not aware that this was a way of coping with his sadness and loss. The particular techniques children use always seem to them to be good solutions to their problems, no matter how foolish, illogical, or self-destructive these actions may appear to adults.

Patterns of Coping

Practitioners need to consider whether a child's coping mode is a way of avoiding or facing stress. Strategies which enable children to go on with their lives without confronting the cause of tension are generally thought to be more useful in the short term. Adaptations which acknowledge and accept the stress are usually deemed to be healthy over the long term.

While there are many ways of avoiding stress, the following four broad categories describe the most typical evasive actions. They are denial, regression, withdrawal, and impulsive acting out. All have both positive and negative consequences for children.

Denial. When using denial, children act as though the stress does not exist. For example, a preschooler goes on playing with her toys while being told that her father has died. Denial serves to alleviate pain and thus can help children preserve their equilibrium. Youngsters may also deny by using fantasy to obliterate reality. They may conjure up imaginary friends to keep them company or rely on magical beliefs to protect themselves and their loved ones.

Regression. When children act younger than their years and engage in earlier behaviors, they are using regression. They become dependent and demanding. As a result, they may receive more physical comforting and affection than usual, thus easing the existing stress.

Withdrawal. In withdrawal children take themselves physically or mentally out of the picture. They run away from the stressful environment or become quiet and almost invisible. They concentrate their attention on pets and inanimate objects or lose themselves in daydreams to escape mentally when they cannot escape physically. Their efforts bring them respite from tension for the time being.

Impulsive Acting Out. Children act impulsively and often flamboyantly to avoid thinking either of the past or of the consequences of their current actions. They conceal their misery by making others angry at them. They seek quick and easy ways to stop their pain. In the process they draw attention to themselves and find ways of momentarily easing their feelings of stress. However, in the long run, this coping strategy is almost guaranteed to be self-destructive.

In contrast to the evasive mechanisms, we can examine five of the many ways in which children accept and face stress. Vaillant (1977) identifies altruism, humor, suppression, anticipation, and sublimation as the *mature mechanisms* which are most used by adult males who are judged effective copers. Children use these strategies too. Again, each has both positive and negative aspects.

Altruism. When children use altruism, they forget their own troubles by helping others, especially parents and siblings. They gain satisfaction from the helper role and from knowing that they are being useful. On the negative side, some altruistic youngsters are more like old men and women than children. They do not allow themselves to be carefree or irresponsible.

Humor. Children joke about their difficulties. They use humor to express anger and pain. When this is taken to its extreme, children lose the ability to cry and to reach out to others for help.

Suppression. Suppression enables children to set aside their anxieties temporarily. For some hours they forget their cares, yet are not afraid to go back to the stressful situation when the free time is over. When there is a death in the family, preschoolers often unconsciously use suppression to maintain their balance. They cry for a while, then go and play as though nothing had happened. Apparently during this time they ignore their pain and gather their strength against the moment when they will return to the adult's side to sob some more. The negative aspect of suppression is that children may suppress feelings to the point of denial.

Anticipation. Children who use anticipation are able to foresee and plan for the next stressful episode. They are then prepared to protect themselves and to accept what cannot be avoided. Anticpation can be a strong coping tool. Its negative aspect is that children may become too fearful and develop compulsive needs to know and plan for what is coming next.

Sublimation. With sublimation, children find ways to vent their anger, overcome their fears, or express their sadness through becoming absorbed in games, sports, and hobbies. These activities become their satisfactions and compensate for the stressful events in their lives. The negative aspect of sublimation is that children can become so engrossed that other pleasures, or the needs of family members can be ignored.

Proposed Helping Strategies

This book proposes that helping professionals use the following three approaches to their work with children under stress. Each can be effective on its own, or they can be applied in combination. These techniques include removal of at least one stressor in a child's life, teaching the youngster new coping strategies, and showing children ways in which they can transfer existing coping techniques to other, more appropriate life situations.

Remove at Least One Stressor. Based on Rutter's (1979) research showing the effects of multiple stresses, it seems reasonable to expect that even a small improvement in the overall situation, that is, the removal of one stress or hassle, can help children to feel stronger and more able. For example, when her teacher arranged a hot breakfast for Lisa (who had been coming to school hungry each morning) the child was then able to concentrate on her schoolwork. This in turn made it possible for Lisa to suppress for a time her anxieties about her parents' impending divorce.

Teach New Coping Strategies. Researchers agree that children who use large repertoires of coping techniques seem to have the best chance of maintaining a healthy equilibrium. When they learn alternative actions, they no longer feel boxed in by fate. For example, Kim was relieved when her social worker helped her to anticipate what it would be like to visit her seriously ill sister. She had been frightened of the hospital and had coped by withdrawing and saying that she didn't want to see her sibling, even though she missed her sister terribly.

Transfer Some Coping Strategies to Other Life Situations. Children tend to apply their coping techniques only to the situations in which they were developed. Adults can show youngsters new ways to use established skills to their best advantage. For example, Jennifer used altruism to cope with her mother's hospitalization for cancer. She coped with the separation by mothering her father, her little brother, and all of her classmates. The children in school quickly got annoyed and began to tease Jennifer. Her teacher helped Jenny to transfer her altruism to taking care of the class pets and being responsible for some daily clean-up chores. The mothering of the other children stopped and so did the teasing.

The three approaches which have been outlined here—removing stressors, teaching new coping strategies, and helping children to transfer existing techniques to other areas of life—can be used by any lay person or professional who works with children. It is, of course, important to be able to recognize when a child will need treatment by a trained therapist. However, considering the large numbers of youngsters who live under stress today, it is equally important that as many adults as possible take responsibility for helping them to cope.

Before Adults Can Help

Effective helpers need a combination of knowledge, appreciation, skill, and self-awareness.

Knowledge. It is important to know as much as possible about the constellation of stressors the child faces, his or her typical coping strategies, and their likely effects on both youngster and family. Workers need to know a variety of alternative actions that might be taken, the legal issues which they must confront, and the community resources which are available.

Appreciation. The helping professional must appreciate children's points of view and their reasons for unconscious choices of coping modes. It is useful to be able to see the stressor through the child's eyes and to understand the good intentions of poor coping mechanisms. The worker needs an appreciation of the complexities of each child's situation and the tangled interactions that can frustrate the most earnest efforts.

Skill. Of course, practitioners need to be skilled in working with children. It is important to be able to communicate easily and warmly with them and, in turn, to gain their trust and to help them to talk openly and completely about their problems.

Self-awareness. A helper's honest awareness of his or her own biases and belief systems in regard to each kind of stressor and each kind of child and family is the fourth requirement.

No matter how adept children become at coping with stress, it is never possible for them to be completely successful; to avoid all negative consequences; and to be able to take everything that comes. Children cannot cope on a daily basis without help and support from at least one caring adult.

References

Belsky, J. 1980. Child maltreatment: An ecological integration. *American Psychologist*, 35:320–335.

Bronfenbrenner, U. 1979. *The ecology of human development*. Cambridge: Harvard University Press.

Bureau of the Census. 1982. *Marital status and living arrangements: March 1982*. Population Characteristics Series P-20, no. 380. Washington, D.C.: Government Printing Office.

Chandler, L.A. 1982. *Children under stress: Understanding emotional adjustment reactions*. Springfield, Ill.: Charles C. Thomas Publisher.

Coddington, R.D. 1972. The significance of life events as etiologic factors in the diseases of children: I—A survey of professional workers. *Journal of Psychosomatic Research*, 16:7–18.

Cohen-Sandler, R., A.L. Berman, and R.A. King. 1982. Life stress and symptomatology: Determinants of suicidal behavior in children. *Journal of the American Academy of Child Psychiatry*, 21:178–186.

Iscoe, I. 1977. *Coping, adaptation and lifestyles*. Modules in Psychology, A-8. Westwood, Mass.: The PaperBook Press.

Kanner, A.D., J.C. Coyne, C. Schaefer, and R.S. Lazarus. 1981. Comparison of two modes of stress measurement: Daily hassles and uplifts versus major life events. *Journal of Behavioral Medicine*, 4:1–39.

Murphy, L.B., and A.E. Moriarty. 1976. *Vulnerability, coping and growth: From infancy to adolescence*. New Haven: Yale University Press.

Rutter, M. 1979. Protective factors in children's responses to stress and disadvantage. In *Primary prevention of psychopathology, Volume III, Social competence in children*, ed. M.W. Kent and J.E. Rolf. Hanover, N.H.: University Press of New England.

Selye, H. 1974. *Stress without distress*. New York: The New American Library, Inc.

Vaillant, G.E. 1977. *Adaptation to life: How the best and the brightest came of age*. Boston: Little, Brown and Company.

2

Stress in Two-Parent Families

The two-parent family is defined as a husband and wife living together with their children. Seventy-five percent of children under fifteen years of age in the United States live in two-parent families (Bureau of the Census 1982). However, this does not necessarily mean that the male parent is the bread-winner and the female is a housewife. That pattern of family life has changed dramatically in the past twelve years. For example, in 1970, only thirty percent of married mothers of children five years old or younger were in the work force. By 1982, forty-nine percent held jobs.

Still, children's lives in two-parent families come as close to normal as any that we will discuss in this book. What then are the sources of stress for these youngsters? The following examples of microsystem, exosystem and macrosystem stresses are meant to illustrate typical problems rather than to be a complete catalog.

Sources of Stress in the Microsystem

Growing Up

A predictable source of stress for children is the fact that they constantly grow and change. No sooner does a family get used to living with their two-year-old than he inexorably moves into a new stage and the family has to find new ways to relate. As much as children want to grow up, it is still a strain for them to recognize that they have indeed developed new abilities which require different levels of planning and judgment.

According to Elkind (1981), this normal stress of growing up is increased when children are hurried into taking on adult behaviors and responsibilities. Elkind believes that today's middle- and upper-class parents push their children to grow up too quickly. These youngsters live under a kind of pressure which has long been felt by lower-class children—the requirement that they become self-sufficient as soon as possible. Elkind maintains that this creates unnecessary stress. Children are urged to learn to read and to excel in school regardless of their readiness for academic tasks. They are encouraged to wear scaled-down versions of adult clothing. Even in summer camp they are expected to polish their hockey skills or learn to program computers. Perhaps the most stressful responsibility that hurried children are asked to undertake is to listen to and share the adults' problems as though they were their parents' contemporaries. Elkind claims that hurried children exhibit many of the symptoms normally associated with stress. They have emotional problems, psychosomatic complaints, appear to be hyperactive or lethargic. They fail in school, become delinquent, and attempt suicide.

New Baby

The birth of a sibling triggers ambivalent feelings of love, hate, protectiveness, and jealousy, that last for the rest of a child's life. According to Bank and Kahn (1982), a consistent new trend is for siblings to be born only a few years apart, so children face the stress of being older brothers and sisters very early in life. Even when the new baby is presented to them as a gift or playmate, they are likely to understand only that they have a competitor whose behavior confuses and irritates them.

Day care arrangements are often made for the two children as a unit. Today, more and more siblings spend their days "alone together." In the absence of their parents, even though a babysitter or other adult may be present, siblings turn to one another for satisfaction, for consistency, and for intimacy. In some cases, they fight with each other as a way of staying in contact and presenting a single front to the outside world (Bank and Kahn 1982).

A further aspect of the sibling relationship develops in these early years. The older child becomes a teacher for the little one. As such, he or she gains a sense of self as an authority and giver of knowledge. Yet, if the younger child is resistant or difficult, the result may be a drastic experience of failure for the big brother or sister.

Fighting

Fighting occurs from time to time even in the most stable and peaceful families. Children are the physical targets of their parents' displeasure, especially if they are considered to be too young to understand verbal reasoning. According to an extensive study by Straus and his colleagues (1980), the majority of parents in the United States use some form of violence on their children at some time in each youngster's life. For most, this takes the form of spanking or slapping, and boys are given physical punishment more often than girls. The researchers found that the more frequently parents spank and slap their youngsters, the more likely the children are to battle with their brothers and sisters and the greater the likelihood that they will hit their parents back. Straus and his associates contend that through intrafamily fighting, children learn that "those who love you the most are also those who hit you," and "those you love are those you hit" (Straus, Gelles, and Steinmetz 1980, 102).

In addition to the stress caused by being physically punished and by their own fights with family members, children become tense when they observe their parents' marital conflicts. They listen to adult voices raised in angry argument and in some cases witness their parents battering one another. These experiences appear to be uniformly frightening to youngsters. Many believe themselves to be the cause of their parents' fights (Barnett et al. 1980). Some cope by trying to draw their parents' attention away from the spousal dispute by misbehaving or getting sick.

Sources of Stress in the Exosystem

New Home

Today's families are highly mobile. Children, on the average, live in two or three different neighborhoods in the course of their first eighteen years (Bank and Kahn 1982). Executive and managerial fathers transfer from city to city, taking their families with them. Blue collar parents are forced to find jobs in new locations when plants close and employment patterns change. Even families which remain in one town move from home to home as their finances dictate. In some cases, the move may represent such severe stress for the parents that the children are at risk of abuse.

Whether the move is across the country or only across town, most parents do little to prepare their children to give up the known environment and old friends. All too frequently, youngsters have no opportunity to help choose or even to visit the new home (Levine 1976). Children tend to identify themselves with specific spaces, repeated events, and familiar people; thus, leaving can cause disorientation. For them, the loss of a place is like the loss of a family member. Yet, within only a few days of their arrival, they are faced with the necessity of finding out who is friendly and who is hostile among the neighbor children. Remembering how hard it was to be the "new kid on the block," some parents help their youngsters to manage this experience with only minor trauma. For others, who are left to cope by themselves, it can be a major source of stress.

For armed forces families, where moves are frequent and children are uprooted every few years, there are official manuals offering suggestions to help youngsters adjust (Department of the Navy 1980). Adults can help children identify their particular skills and use them to gain recognition in the new community

keep a scrapbook of children's achievements to look back on when they are feeling lost after a move

teach children sports they can do alone so they can keep active while waiting for school to start

begin in nursery school to help children learn how to make new friends easily

enroll children in scouts or other national organizations so they can rejoin immediately in the new community

School

Even if they live in the same house all of their lives, most children enter a new school at least once before they reach puberty. Each year in the fall there are new classrooms, teachers, and demands for coping and adaptation.

School is the child's first world of his own; it is one in which parents cannot participate and which siblings share only at a distance. Some children experience this as a separation from their families and consequently a stressful event. Others leave their homes quite comfortably. There is considerable stress however for any youngster in the process of establishing his or her personal reputation with teachers and peers. All have to find ways to fit themselves into the existing classroom milieu and to learn the system for getting what they want from each school day. Levine (1976) has found that children from highly mobile families have the most difficulty in entering classroom social systems. They tend to remain isolated. Teachers often go out of their way to welcome new children. Some have developed strategies which allow youngsters to stay on the sidelines and observe or to rehearse the way in which they plan to join the group.

School is also the place where children are faced with their first decisions about obeying or breaking the law. As far back as 1976, a survey by the firm of Yankelovich, Skelly and White, found that the majority of elementary school children said they were personally acquainted with youngsters who had broken the law, had been picked up by the police, and/or had stolen things. One in four ten-to-twelve-year-olds reported that they knew children who had tried marijuana or other drugs. Children whose mothers worked were somewhat more likely to claim knowledge of runaways or youngsters who had broken the law (General Mills American Family Report 1976–77).

Current experience suggests that the number of children who use drugs, who steal, and who run away from home, have increased since 1977. Children watch their classmates break the law and then must cope with the stress of making decisions for themselves about these issues. Often they are under pressure from their peers and make their choices without the knowledge or help of adult family members.

Working Parents

When both parents work, arrangements for the care of their children are central to the way in which the family functions. Every week there are periods of time when children must be cared for by others or left on their own. Even the best child care arrangements involve stress for children and their parents. Everybody in the family has to adjust to living on a schedule. Lein (1979) found that most of the parents she studied had high standards for their children's care and were willing to change their working hours rather than compromise these goals. They made elaborate agreements so that fathers and mothers were away from home at different hours. They used as little out-of-home care as possible. Under these circumstances, she found that fathers generally ignored the housework and spent their time at home playing with the children. Mothers handled chores and child-minding simultaneously. Obviously, time spent with mother was more stressful for the children than the hours with father.

Older boys and girls frequently put pressure on working mothers to become more like the stereotypical housewife (Skinner 1980). They apparently feel some stress in having a parent who is different from society's role model. At the same time, there is evidence that girls benefit from having working mothers. They seem to admire independence and to seek to emulate their mothers (Crouter 1982).

Many professional parents have to take time away from their families for business travel. Studies of the children of male executives show that there is stress in having a father who is chronically absent from home. His long working day and trips which keep him away for several nights at a time are sources of strain for his children (Voydanoff 1980). While nobody has yet studied mothers who have executive positions, it seems likely that their youngsters respond similarly to their mother's absences from home.

The general concensus of research on working parents is that most increase their own feelings of stress as they attempt to juggle complex schedules. Their children sense and are affected by these tensions. In addition, the youngsters feel stress as they adapt to a series of child care providers (Skinner 1980).

Workaholic Parents

Another category of working parents love their children but place their own career ambitions first. Braun calls these couples workaholics and defines them as parents "whose career ambitions require a total commitment to work and/or study as a matter of personal choice" (Braun 1980, 7). When their jobs or studies demand more time and concentration, they may lower their standards for domestic tasks and child care. They are likely to purchase supervision for their children, hire domestic help, and buy mechanical gadgets to speed up housekeeping chores. Workaholics never stop working. A game of Monopoly with the children may be interrupted time after time as Mom telephones her colleagues and Dad writes notes to himself for tomorrow's conference.

Because parents are trying to fit more into each day than can be accomplished, children of workaholics do a lot of waiting. They wait for the carpool and for the sitter. They wait for Mom to finish her staff meeting. They wait for Dad's plane to land. They wait until their parents can schedule time to be with them. They have little control over their own lives. A few become so distressed with this that, even in school, they cannot participate in activities, but spend the hours waiting to go home.

In their attempts to obtain their workaholic parents' undivided attention, children behave in ways that increase the family's level of stress. They become slower at dressing and getting ready to leave the house. They throw temper tantrums at the sight of a babysitter. Their dramatic reactions to their workaholic parents serve to increase tension for everybody.

Unemployed Parents

In contrast to living with workaholic parents, daily life in families where there is an unemployed spouse can be relatively calm. Particularly when a parent perceives him or herself to be in the process of changing jobs rather than out of work, there is little stress for family members. In such situations, one out of ten fathers and mothers report that their relationship with their children actually improves when they are not working (Thomas, McCabe, and Berry 1980).

Similarly, the first few weeks after a parent has been laid off can be free of stress even if there is little hope of immediately finding another job.

During this period there is usually a cushion of unemployment benefits and little stigma in being one of the millions in the United States who are out of work.

However, the effects of long-term unemployment are more stressful for children. As the tension level increases for their parents, youngsters feel the effects. This is especially true when the parent becomes depressed by futile job hunting efforts. Ferman (1979) found that although there is little strain at the time of initial job loss, tension increases as the individual searches for work and is turned away. The greatest stress occurs in families where a parent is hired, works for several weeks or months, and is laid off or fired for a second time.

Unemployment can become the central theme in family life. When the youngsters have problems, rather than attributing them to the child's personality or stage of development, parents blame their own lack of money and their absorption with job hunting (Cunningham 1983). Because they are spending more time at home, adults come to depend on their sons and daughters for a kind of emotional support that is beyond their children's years (Ferman 1979). The lack of money for babysitters can enforce constant contact with youngsters which becomes overwhelming (Cordes 1983).

Children respond to parental unemployment with ambivalence. They resent the loss of the things that money used to buy. At the same time, they want to help and to make everything right again for Mom and Dad. Older boys and girls hunt for ways to add to the family's income. In some communities this has led to direct conflicts with jobless adults who have taken the traditional children's jobs of mowing lawns and shoveling snow. Some youngsters turn to petty theft. They shoplift toys and clothing or take quarters from their parents' dresser tops to play their favorite arcade games (Cordes 1983).

In too many cases, parents fail to explain the effects their job loss will have on the family's style of living and their children become confused and frightened. Cordes' (1983) study of Detroit's unemployed found that most youngsters' greatest fear was that they would be evicted from their homes and have their belongings dumped onto the sidewalk. The majority said they had seen neighbors put out of their homes.

The most serious effects of long-term unemployment appear to be felt in the areas of maternal and child health. According to Michigan's Senator Donald W. Riegle, Jr., the infant mortality rate, which had been decreasing during the previous decade, began to rise as unemployment skyrocketed in his state. Michigan researchers found that children whose parents were unemployed frequently had upset stomachs and were irritable. In some cases their physical and mental development slowed down. According to Senator Riegle, "During the past year, the number of children receiving psychological counseling because of problems related to their parents' unemployment has risen nearly 30% at Children's Hospital of Michigan" (Riegle 1982, 1114–1115).

Sources of Stress in the Macrosystem

Racial and Religious Prejudice

Macrosystem attitudes toward the racial and religious group to which a child belongs can create pride or shame. Youngsters discover what society thinks and feels about their ethnic group through the media and through the treatment they receive from adults and peers. Sometimes the picture is complimentary. More often, cultural differences are presented as laughable deviants from the norm through ethnic jokes and the plots of television situation comedies.

In their attempts to protect their children from stereotyping and prejudice, minority parents often demand that they excel in school or in sports and aim for professional careers. In comparison with other children, more minority youngsters report that their parents have high expectations for them in daily activities in and out of school (General Mills American Family Report 1976–77). Parents also pressure their children to pay extra attention to clothing and grooming on the assumption that well-dressed youngsters are treated better.

Quite early in life minority children realize that they are not one but two people living in the same body. They are simultaneously American and a member of a unique subgroup (Silverstein and Krate 1975). Frequently, the significant adults in children's lives outside of their families are members of the majority culture. Teachers and school principals, police who patrol the neighborhood, salespeople in local stores, team coaches and playground supervisors, are predominantly Caucasian and Christian. Youngsters depend on these adults for fair treatment and at the same time know that in many cases they are regarded first as Blacks, Jews, Hispanics, or Orientals, and second as individuals. Compared to majority children, Blacks, for example, know that there is a greater chance that their teachers will pick on them for minor rule infractions and expel or suspend them from school for major ones (Edelman 1980).

In addition to living with prejudicial treatment by adults, minority children face the threat of physical abuse, scapegoating, and verbal abuse from their peers. They soon learn that the number of potential friends they have in school is limited first to children of their own race or religion and second to a few of the members of the majority. Throughout childhood they live with the stress of being partly acceptable and partly outside of the mainstream.

Poverty

Perhaps the most severe of the ordinary life stresses faced by children are those which result from being poor. More than 10,120,000 children in the United States today live in poverty. Seven percent of all families with children under the age of eighteen live below the poverty level (Bureau of the Census 1980). This means that there are more than ten million children in this country who often go to bed hungry, who live in substandard housing, and who receive little or no health care.

The stresses are somewhat different for children in families where poverty is a chronic condition as compared with those where income has suddenly been reduced. This second group of the newly poor is composed of parents who had, until recently, been providing adequately for their children. Many still own homes and now have to choose between paying the mortgage and buying food. Their children must quickly adjust to a lower standard of living and to being dependent on welfare programs or charity. They experience the stress of watching their parents' humiliation at standing in line for free food and accepting donations of used clothing. Some apparently resort to stealing, since large city supermarkets report that increases in the number of young children caught pilfering food from their shelves correlates with rising unemployment (Schoen 1983).

Data from the depression of the 1930s suggest that at least in those days, a period of temporary poverty for a family was weathered better by girls than by boys. Studies of children who were toddlers at the beginning of the 1930s show that hostility developed between boys and their fathers when a formerly middle class family lived in poverty for a few years. As they reached adolescence, these young males had a sense that they had been victimized by society. On the other hand, girls of the same age developed strong ties with their mothers; were less affected by both parents' unpredictable and sometimes sullen behavior; and reached adolescence as goal-oriented, assertive young women. Most had observed their mothers becoming successful breadwinners as well as homemakers as the depression deepened (Elder 1979).

In contrast with the newly poor, chronically poor families bring up their children in an environment where the two major causes of stress are inadequate nutrition and nonexistent health care. The effects of both are felt even before the child is born. They last throughout childhood. Most low income parents have too little cash to shop in large supermarkets where the middle class takes advantage of coupons and special sales. Many find they have to buy food each day in small quantities in local stores where they can buy on credit at higher prices. The result is less and lower quality food for poor children. Teachers in poverty areas report that youngsters often come to school hungry and there is a lack of government-funded breakfast and lunch programs to ease restlessness and irritability. Most experts agree that hunger decreases children's ability to learn.

Often free medical clinics are located at some distance from the neighborhoods in which poor families live. Parents in rural areas may have to travel for many miles to find these services. The cost of transportation, babysitters for younger siblings, and time off from a job make it difficult or impossible for many mothers and fathers to take their children to these centers. The Children's Defense Fund estimates that "ten million children, or one in six, get virtually no health care whatsoever and thus do not get the regular checkups that parents naturally want for their children" (Edelman 1981, 110). Poor youngsters learn to cope with the distress of untreated toothaches, recurring colds and flu, broken eyeglasses worn taped together, and a myriad of pains and symptoms that receive no care.

Sharff (1981) studied chronically poor Hispanic families living in an urban area scarred by burned-out buildings, drug dealing, street violence, and a high death rate among its young men. She found that these families tried to insure their survival by socializing their children into specific roles. One boy or girl might become a legitimate wage earner early in life. Another boy might act as a protector of his younger siblings and eventually learn the trade of drug dealer or thief in order to bring in additional income. Sharff labeled another role as that of *scholar/advocate*. In her study this was sometimes a boy, but more often a girl. The girl spoke for her parents at the welfare agency and in the school principal's office. She interpreted to her parents the fine points of the macrosystem's rules. The family pinned their hopes on her ability to grow up to use her intelligence and assertiveness to move out of poverty and into a pink collar job. Each of these roles was stressful for the child, yet each had its compensation in being recognized as important by other family members.

How Children Learn to Cope

For millions of children in two-parent families, the stresses discussed in this chapter are the normal tensions of growing up. The children are not taught how to cope, yet somehow they learn. They use the resources of the microsystem (strategies they devise for themselves, advice of parents and siblings), the teachings of the exosystem (influences of teachers, religious leaders, neighbors, and friends), and the subtle messages abroad in the macrosystem (television and other media, interactions with institutions). Of these informal ways in which children learn to cope with stress, only those in the macrosystem, and specifically in television programming, have been studied in detail. In recent years research has demonstrated that children learn facts and attitudes, and their behavior is shaped by what they see and hear on television (National Institute of Mental Health 1982).

Among children's incidental learnings from television are a group of coping strategies that TV characters employ to deal with tension. Some of these are ways of facing stress, for example, prosocial behaviors; and others are techniques of avoidance, including the use of alcohol and impulsive acting out.

Facing Stress: Prosocial Behavior

A number of controlled studies have shown that children learn to be more generous, friendly, and self-controlled by watching specific programs which are designed to teach prosocial coping behaviors. Apparently, these shows are more effective when adults reinforce the prosocial message by encouraging children to discuss or act out what they have seen. For example, pupils who acted out a situation they saw on the "Mister Rogers Neighborhood" show incorporated their new knowledge into subsequent behavior. In the program, a little girl was taught how to cope with her fear that she would lose her friends to a new child who had entered the class. Immediately following the show, the children role-played the characters and the situation. Later, when new youngsters joined their class, it was clear that the children had learned a prosocial way to cope with them (National Institute of Mental Health 1982).

Television watching in itself has been thought of as a way of reducing stress. Using the coping technique of suppression, it can be a way to avoid thinking about a stressful event—at least for the moment. Studies show that if the content of the program being viewed is not related to the existing stress, then television can help a child to unwind and relax (National Institute of Mental Health 1982).

Avoiding Stress

Use of Alcohol. The National Institute of Mental Health report (1982) quotes studies which indicate that in a day of television viewing, most children see at least ten instances of adults drinking alcoholic beverages. Often this is heavy drinking of five or more beers or whiskies. In most of these televised episodes, alcohol is portrayed as a way of relieving tension. Thus, children learn that alcohol is a socially approved method of reducing stress.

Impulsive Acting Out. By far the greatest number of studies have focused on the issue of whether or not children learn aggressive behavior by watching television. Eron (1982) finds that youngsters become more aggressive after witnessing violence on television. He also contends that agressive youngsters choose to watch violent programs more frequently than other children. Eron proposes this as a circular phenomenon. Boys and girls who do poorly in school and have few friends spend more time watching television than high-achieving, popular children. Low achievers identify with the aggressive men and women who are their favorite TV characters, and are likely to imitate the observed tactics when they deal with their classmates. Their increased aggressiveness makes them even less popular than before and they have more time to watch TV.

Children Who Cope Effectively

Most children in normal two-parent families can be expected to arrive at adulthood in reasonably good mental health—able to work well, play well, and remain hopeful—despite the stresses to which they have been exposed. Obviously, such youngsters are able to devise their own effective ways of adapting to tension and crisis. In their longitudinal study of resilient children, Werner and Smith (1982) found a cluster of personality traits and coping techniques that were characteristic of children who grew into adulthood with relatively few emotional scars despite childhood stress. These youngsters were generally active, good-natured, affectionate, and socially adept. They were better than their age-mates at caring for their own needs and controlling their own impulses. They were able to concentrate on a task, get absorbed in a special interest or hobby, and had good feelings about themselves. In addition, the resilient children had some important sources of support in the micro- and exosystems. They received positive attention from caregivers in addition to their parent(s), especially during the first years of their lives. Their homes were structured and had rules and shared values.

The Werner and Smith study (1982) can serve to indicate goals for helping professionals who are attempting to assist more vulnerable children. Their clients may need to develop some of the characteristics and be given some of the adult supports typical of resilient children. Hopefully, this will enable them to cope more effectively with the ordinary life stresses of growing up in two-parent families.

References

Bank, S.P., and M.D. Kahn. 1982. *The sibling bond.* New York: Basic Books, Inc., Publishers.

Barnett, E.R., C.B. Pittman, C.K. Ragan, and M.K. Salus. 1980. *Family violence: Intervention strategies.* National Center on Child Abuse and Neglect, (OHDS) 80–30258. Washington, D.C.: Government Printing Office.

Braun, S.J. 1980. Some family matters that affect young children. *BAEYC Reports,* 22:3–10.

Bureau of the Census. 1980. *Provisional estimates of social, economic, and housing characteristics, 1980 census of population and housing.* Supplementary Report, PHC80–51–1. Washington, D.C.: Government Printing Office.

―――. 1982. *Marital status and living arrangements, March 1982.* Population Characteristics, Ser. P–20, no. 380. Washington, D.C.: Government Printing Office.

Cordes, C. 1983. Detroit: A ravaged city copes with the human toll. *Monitor,* American Psychological Association. January.

Crouter, A.C. 1982. The children of working parents. *Children Today,* July-August.

Cunningham, S. 1983. Shock of layoff felt deep inside family circle. *Monitor,* American Psychological Association, January.

Department of the Navy. 1980. *Making a home in the Navy: Ideas to grow on.* The Family Support Program Branch (OP-152). Washington, D.C.

Edelman, M.W. 1980. *Portrait of inequality: Black and white children in America.* Washington, D.C.: Children's Defense Fund.

―――. 1981. Who is for children? *American Psychologist,* 36:109–116.

Elder, G.H. 1979. Families in hard times―a legacy. In *Families today: A research sampler on families and children, Volume 1,* ed. E. Corfman, NIMH. Washington, D.C.: Government Printing Office.

Elkind, D. 1981. *The hurried child: Growing up too fast too soon.* Reading, Mass.: Addison-Wesley Publishing Company.

Eron, L.D. 1982. Parent-child interaction, television violence, and aggression of children. *American Psychologist,* 37:197–211.

Ferman, L. 1979. Family adjustment to unemployment. In *Families today: A research sampler on families and children, Volume 1,* ed. E. Corfman, NIMH. Washington, D.C.: Government Printing Office.

Fried, M. 1976. Grieving for a lost home. In *Human adaptation: Coping with life crises,* ed. R.H. Moos. Lexington, Mass.: Lexington Books, D.C. Heath and Company.

General Mills American Family Report. 1976–77. *Raising children in a changing society.* Minneapolis: General Mills, Inc.

Lein, L. 1979. Working couples as parents. In *Families today: A research sampler on families and children, Volume 1,* ed. E. Corfman, NIMH. Washington, D.C.: Government Printing Office.

Levine, M. 1976. Residential change and school adjustment. In *Human adaptation: Coping with life crises,* ed. R.H. Moos. Lexington, Mass.: Lexington Books, D.C. Heath and Company.

National Institute of Mental Health. 1982. *Television and behavior: Ten years of scientific progress and implications for the eighties.* Volume I, Summary Report (ADM)82-1195. Washington, D.C.: Government Printing Office.

Riegle, D.W., Jr. 1982. The psychological and social effects of unemployment. *American Psychologist,* 37:1113–1115.

Schoen, E. 1983. Once again, hunger troubles America. *The New York Times Magazine,* January 2.

Sharff, J.W. 1981. Free enterprise and the ghetto family. *Psychology Today,* March.

Silverstein, B., and R. Krate. 1975. *Children of the dark ghetto: A developmental psychology.* New York: Praeger Publishers.

Skinner, D.A. 1980. Dual-career family stresss and coping: a literature review. *Family Relations,* 29:473–480.

Straus, M.A., R.J. Gelles, and S.K. Steinmetz. 1980. *Behind closed doors: Violence in the American family.* Garden City, N.Y.: Anchor Press/Doubleday.

Thomas, L.E., E. McCabe, and J.E. Berry. 1980. Unemployment and family stress: A reassessment. *Family Relations,* 29:517–524.

U.S. Congress. House. 1983. Select Committee on Children, Youth, and Families. *U.S. children and their families: Current conditions and recent trends.* 98th Cong. 1st sess. Committee Print.

Voydanoff, P. 1980. Work roles as stressors in corporate families. *Family Relations,* 29:489–494.

Werner, E.E., and R.S. Smith. 1982. *Vulnerable but invincible: A longitudinal study of resilient children and youth.* New York: McGraw-Hill Book Company.

3 Stress in One-Parent Families

One in every five children under the age of fifteen in the United States lives with a single parent. Of these, 10,244,000 live with their mothers and 896,000 with their fathers. Most single parents were previously married but are now separated, divorced, or widowed. However, 1,759,000 children live with mothers and 104,000 with fathers who have never married (Bureau of the Census 1982). A growing proportion of unmarried mothers are teenagers.

One-parent households come in as many varieties as two-parent domiciles. The single parent may live alone with his/her children or may share the home with one or more related or unrelated adults. The single parent may range in age from adolescence to middle adulthood and have a great deal of money or be living below the poverty level. He or she may be well-educated or a school dropout; work sixty hours a week or be unemployed; be an excellent parent or a failure. Society generally ignores this enormous variety and expects that single parents will be less successful in raising their children than couples. Current research on the risks of growing up with one parent provides us with little help in evaluating the validity of this belief. Blechman's (1982) survey of research methodology labels the results of most studies as inconclusive. Without careful comparison of one-parent as compared with matched groups of two-parent children whose families have similar education and income levels, she believes that psychologists cannot draw firm conclusions. She maintains that there are no studies which prove that children need two parents of opposite gender in order to become well-adjusted adults.

Basically, children in one-parent households share the same stresses as their two-parent contemporaries. In addition, they face a group of stressors which are peculiar to their status. For them, some microsystem stress arises from the presence or absence of extra adults in their homes. Another group of stresses may develop if they are treated as equals by their single parents. They also face macrosystem stresses caused by the expectations that society holds for one-parent families.

Sources of Stress

Adults in the Household

Whether they are headed by a mother or a father, many one-parent households contain additional adults. A study by Kellam and his colleagues (1982) found single mothers living with their own parents, grandmothers, aunts, and unrelated adults. Teenage mothers often started out by living with their own parents. By the time they had their second child, at least half, although still unmarried, had established their own homes and lived alone with their youngsters. Where there was a second adult present in the home, the nurturant role taken by that individual appeared to be crucial for the child's functioning. Kellam and his associates found that youngsters who lived with a mother and a grandmother seemed to be better adjusted in school and more stable psychologically than those whose homes included other categories of resident adults. Apparently, some kinds of live-in adults create stress in the parent-child relationship rather than provide support and stability.

Role Equality

Being a single parent is a lonely job and it is natural for Mom or Dad to turn to the children for companionship. Sometimes the relationship becomes so close that the roles of parent and child seem to merge. When they are asked to help with decisions about family finances or whether or not the parent should go out on a date, children have been elevated to equal status with the adult. This is not role reversal, because youngsters do not become caregivers to their parents. Instead, they become equal partners in the adult role, in some ways filling the place of the missing spouse. This creates both positive and negative stress. On the one hand, they enjoy being equals and, on the other, they miss being treated as children.

When they think back, one-parent children report that it was great to be needed and to be a contributing member of the household. At the same time they were dismayed to discover that their mother or father couldn't cope very well; that he or she was vulnerable, perhaps unreliable, even foolish. They were inwardly pleased to be depended upon as sympathetic listeners, but grew to resent lost playtime with friends. They felt older and more self-confident than their peers in school and looked down on two-parent children as spoiled babies.

Some psychologists maintain that by taking on adult responsibilities so early in life, these youngsters have forfeited any chance of fulfilling their natural desires to be treated as children. Weiss (1981) contends that they can only gain their parents' attention by acting as role equals and denying their dependency needs. He goes on to claim that such youngsters may cope with the stress of heavy home burdens by becoming withdrawn and making few friends outside of their immediate families.

Sex Roles

As boys and girls reach the ages of ten and eleven, society puts pressure on single parents to find role models to substitute for the missing spouse. Even adults who believe in equality of the sexes find themselves pressured to enroll their children in clubs where they can be in weekly contact with a same-sex leader. Social workers assign youngsters to "big brothers" or "big sisters" with similar goals in mind. Mothers in particular face the stigma of creating potential homosexuals if they don't provide their prepubertal sons with adult male companionship and training in sports. Single fathers are expected to have difficulty in preparing their daughters for menstruation and in helping them to acquire feminine mannerisms. While children enjoy their contact with extrafamily sex role models, there is also stress in knowing that the world at large considers their parents deficient in providing them with the kind of home that every American child is supposed to have.

Life with Father versus Life with Mother

There is some evidence that life with a single father may be less stressful than life with a single mother. Smith and Smith (1981) report that single fathers are more easygoing with their children when they have sole responsibility for their upbringing. Orthner and his associates (1976) found that single fathers devoted more time to their children after gaining custody. Whether his children have been born in or out wedlock, a man usually must demonstrate to a judge that he can support them financially and emotionally and that he will be a better parent than their mother before he will be awarded custody (Orthner, Brown, and Ferguson 1976). Thus, single fathers are likely to be employed and to have reasonably steady incomes. Society has high regard for a man who brings up his children without a wife.

Single mothers, on the other hand, face social disapproval in many areas. For example, they have more difficulty in finding decent housing. Landlords throughout the country discriminate against female-headed families (Children's Defense Fund 1981). Children have to live in substandard dwellings and less desirable neighborhoods simply because their mothers are unmarried. Often these are high crime areas as well (Dill et al. 1980). In school, youngsters may be the butt of peer taunts that their mothers can't find or can't keep husbands, or that they are prostitutes.

In summary, the differences in the amount of stress experienced by children who live with single fathers as compared with single mothers may be caused more by the family's socioeconomic status than by the parent's sex (Ambert 1982; McLanahan 1983).

Life on Welfare

Two and a half million single mothers today struggle to bring up their children on incomes below the poverty level (Bureau of the Census 1980). Most depend on welfare assistance for food, clothing, and shelter. And because they subsist on public money, they are frequently at the mercy of institutional rules. Solutions to even the most ordinary household problems require a tremendous effort when agency regulations govern the money that a mother can spend. It may take weeks or months of red tape and numerous visits to the welfare office to secure a crib for a newborn, to get a broken refrigerator fixed, or to get permission for a child's dental work. Under these circumstances, family members come to feel powerless.

Mothers who are continually blocked and frustrated by the cumbersome welfare system tend to blame themselves rather than the bureaucracy (Dill et al. 1980). As a result, they succumb to what some psychologists call *learned helplessness*. Their experiences teach them that they cannot, despite their best efforts, achieve their goals for their families. Some give up and become depressed. Belle (1980) found that during periods of depression, women have difficulty in being good parents to their children. They are less able to accept ordinary childish actions and overreact to minor misbehavior by yelling at and hitting their youngsters. Their children report being under stress and unhappy during their mother's periods of depression.

Most welfare families have a social worker assigned to them. This dual authority is a source of stress for children when the beliefs of mother and social worker conflict.

Another cause of tension occurs when classmates know about a family's dependence on welfare. Youngsters believe that society looks down on poor people, calls them lazy, and says that they wouldn't be in this fix if they were willing to work hard. Many feel ashamed of being poor. Christina, for example, remembers with irony how happy she was when her social worker brought her a new coat. The next day she burst into tears when she walked into the schoolyard and saw that all of the girls in her class whose families were on welfare had received identical garments.

Barriers to Learning How to Cope

Children in one-parent households use many of the same coping strategies as those who grow up with two parents. However, they are likely to face several unique barriers which may keep them from learning effective ways of adapting to stress. For example, it is common for one-parent youngsters to have fantasies about their missing fathers or mothers. They imagine that life with the absent parent would be far better than their current lot. Some live for years with an unfounded expectation that a nonexistent parent will turn up and give them all the things they need. As a result, they fail to make realistic coping efforts.

Children who live alone with their single parent often share that adult's isolation and lack of contact with relatives and adult friends who might serve as resources in learning to cope. Kellam and his colleagues (1982) found that sixty percent of mothers who live alone with their youngsters are isolated. With only their mothers to share ideas and daily exploits, and no other adults to take them places or play with them, these children learn a limited repertoire of coping techniques. They lack the advantage of an additional parent or other live-in adult from whom they can absorb a variety of strategies.

Another barrier to the development of effective coping skills is learned helplessness. If their low-income mothers have struggled in vain to provide for the family's basic needs, children learn that even heroic attempts to solve problems are futile.

In many cases, one-parent children find themselves stereotyped by their teachers who expect them to be less happy, less well-adjusted, and less able to cope with stress than two-parent youngsters (Santrock and Tracy 1978). Teachers who set lower standards for pupils known to have home problems, begin a downward spiral in the academic goals which these children set for themselves.

Youngsters who live in neighborhoods where they see crime, violence, and drug dealing as they walk to and from school are likely to learn coping skills on the street which are vastly different from those taught in the classroom. As a result they have little respect for well-meaning instructors who try to teach them to discuss rather than fight and who then go safely home to the suburbs after school. These boys and girls know that without their fists and wits they will not survive on the street. They erect what seem to them to be realistic barriers to learning coping strategies from school personnel.

Television provides little assistance to one-parent children. Situation comedies and soap operas portray such families in highly unrealistic ways. In the space of a half-hour, life's most difficult crises are resolved to everybody's satisfaction. These offerings feed into children's fantasies about an idealized world where any goal can be reached without effort. In addition, they reinforce the certainty that there is something wrong with the children and their single parent because they can't manage their lives the way the characters do on television. The children's resulting loss of self-esteem becomes another barrier to learning to cope with stress.

Helping Single-Parent Children Cope

Clearly, some of the barriers which prevent children from learning how to cope with stress can be removed by adults committed to helping these youngsters. While missing-parent fantasies may need the expert skill of a therapist before they disappear, other barriers are amenable to straightforward attack. For example, when a teacher's expectations for a child appear to be set too low, a series of conferences can be scheduled to explore the strengths which exist despite the child's family problems. Teacher, helper, and child (if old enough) can plan together to overcome academic deficiencies and set realistic goals for higher achievement.

Isolation is another barrier which can be broken. To help children of working parents, the American Association of University Women in State College, Pennsylvania, set up a Phone Friend service. Youngsters who return from school to an empty house or apartment and are lonely, fearful, or in need of an adult's advice, can telephone a widely advertised number. Trained volunteers talk with the callers and temporarily relieve their sense of isolation (Goodman 1983).

A more permanent way of dealing with children's lack of companions is to help them to make friends not only with peers but with adult neighbors, storekeepers, and the employees of local businesses. A network of adult friends can provide coping models and a variety of ideas and points of view.

References

Ambert, A. 1982. Differences in children's behavior toward custodial mothers and custodial fathers. *Journal of Marriage and the Family*, 44:73–86.

Belle, D. 1980. Summary and conclusion. In *Lives in stress: A context for depression*, ed. D. Belle, Stress and Families Project. Cambridge: Harvard School of Education. Mimeo.

Blechman, E.A. 1982. Are children of one parent at psychological risk? A methodological review. *Journal of Marriage and the Family*, 44:179–195.

Bureau of the Census. 1980. *Provisional estimates of social, economic, and housing characteristics, 1980 census of population and housing*. Supplementary Report, PHC80–51–1. Washington, D.C.: Government Printing Office.

————. 1982. *Marital status and living arrangements, March 1982*. Population Characteristics, Ser. P–20, no. 380. Washington, D.C.: Government Printing Office.

Children's Defense Fund. 1981. *A brief overview of housing discrimination against families with children*. Washington, D.C.: Children's Defense Fund.

Dill, D., E. Feld, J. Martin, S. Beukema, and D. Belle. 1980. The impact of the environment on the coping efforts of low-income mothers. *Family Relations*, 29:503–509.

Goodman, H. 1983. Dial-A-Friend. *Psychology Today*, June.

Kellam, S.G., R.G. Adams, C.H. Brown, and M.E. Ensminger. 1982. The long-term evolution of the family structure of teenage and older mothers. *Journal of Marriage and the Family*, 44:539–554.

McLanahan, S.S. 1983. Family structure and stress: A longitudinal comparison of two-parent and female-headed families. *Journal of Marriage and the Family*, 45:347–357.

Orthner, D.K., T. Brown, and D. Ferguson. 1976. Single-parent fatherhood: An emerging family life style. *The Family Coordinator*, 25:429–437.

Santrock, J.W., and R.W. Tracy, 1978. Effects of children's family structure status on the development of stereotypes by teachers. *Journal of Educational Psychology*, 70:754–757.

Smith, R.M., and C.W. Smith. 1981. Child rearing and single-parent fathers. *Family Relations*, 30:411–417.

Weiss, R.S. 1981. Growing up a little faster: Children in single-parent households. *Children Today*, May–June.

4

Stress in Multiparent Families

Multiple-Parent, Multiple-Dwelling Families

Imagine a child who has two fathers (one biological, one step) and two mothers (one biological, one step). Both pairs of parents maintain separate homes and the child lives with each for a portion of the year. In addition, this youngster has eight grandparents (four biological, four step), biological siblings, stepsiblings (some belonging to the stepfather, some to the stepmother), and perhaps one or two half-siblings born to the remarried couples. Add to these an assortment of aunts, uncles, and cousins related to the two fathers and two mothers and a picture begins to form of the complexity of a typical multiparent family. Some relationships are even more convoluted when there has been more than one remarriage for either or both of the child's biological parents. The category of multiparent family also includes live-in lovers (heterosexual or homosexual) and their children. It is estimated that one out of every five children in the United States lives in some variation of the multiparent family (Einstein 1980).

As is the case with one-parent children, these youngsters share all of the basic stresses found in the traditional two-parent family. In addition they face a spectrum of stresses unique to their multiparent status. Studies of remarried couples who have sought help with their own and their children's adjustment problems provide descriptions of tensions within the compound family (microsystem), in relations with schools and peers (exosystem), and in dealings with the outside world, particularly the courts (macrosystem).

Stress in the Microsystem

New Relationships. When Mom or Dad remarries, the children are forced to give up their cherished fantasies that their biological parents will get together again. The old family is dead, and children grieve for it during the first weeks and months of the new one. Often they are under stress because they are expected to adjust quickly to the stepfamily without any period of mourning. Children also tend to believe that they were happier in the earlier nuclear family or when they lived alone with their single parent (Wald 1981). This can make it more difficult for them to accept the members of their new stepfamily. In too many cases, both children and parents expect that marriage will create instant love among the members. Yet, each has come to the new home with an established history of ways of behaving which is resistant to change. The reality is likely to be constant friction over opposing sets of manners and mores—a painful experience for all. Thus, the first weeks and months of a remarriage are usually a period of stress.

Youngsters have a natural fear that this marriage too will fail or that this parent too will die; that the child's investment in loving another adult will end in separation and loss. There is some measure of reality in this fear, since more than forty percent of second marriages end in divorce before the couple's fifth anniversary (Einstein 1980).

Right from the start, the most urgent question that children ask about their new family relates to terms of address. "Must I call him Daddy?" "Do I say Roger is my brother or do I tell the kids he's my stepbrother?" "Why do I have a different last name from everybody else in the family?" Children must continually make decisions about titles for the members of their new step-families. Because of the implied level of equality, they may be quite uncomfortable calling stepparents by their first names, yet there are no accepted common or endearing titles for members of a multifamily. Some children cope with this problem by never using names at all.

Another major issue is authority. Who has the right to tell which children what to do? If the family does not work as a unit to discuss lines of authority and establish mutually acceptable rules and regulations, there can be considerable stress for the children. Without these agreements, they are torn between the values of one spouse as opposed to the other and between loyalty to the biological parent and growing love and respect for the new adult in the family.

Children are concerned too about the changes in their relationships with their biological parents. They miss the experience of having their Mom or Dad all to themselves. It is similarly stressful to watch their mother devote most of her time to efforts to win the love of the stepchildren. Youngsters who were treated as role equals by adults during the years between marriages may be shocked and angry to find themselves relegated to the status of children again.

The custodial parent's remarriage always results in a move to a new home, school, and neighborhood for at least one set of children in the blended family. Those whose school careers and friendships are disrupted may deeply resent that their parent's happiness has resulted in their own lives being torn apart.

Yet, the noncustodial parent's remarriage may be even more distressing. According to Warshak and Santrock (1983), many children express negative feelings when their noncustodial parent acquires a new mate and family. They suggest that this second alliance may seem to the youngsters to threaten to break the already fragile ties to a loved one with whom they have infrequent contact.

The Cinderella Role. It is not clear how children cope with the stress which they experience as they move into multiparent families. Some psychologists theorize that they displace their anger, frustration, fear, and anxiety from the biological parent to the stepparent (Einstein 1980). Whatever the dynamics, studies show that friction between children and their stepparents and fights among stepsiblings create the most stress in remarried households (Wald 1981). Children do not automatically love their parent's lover and many years of living together may pass before they express any affection or respect. Each youngster has a biological parent who permeates his thoughts and directs his behavior even though that individual is miles away or no longer living. On the other hand, when the step bond becomes close and supportive, it can be a potent force for growth in children, leading to good adjustment in school and increased capacity to cope with problems (Furstenberg 1983).

Biological siblings may attempt to deal with their insecurities in the new family by forming coalitions against the stepchildren, leading to intrafamily warfare. When this happens, home changes from a place of safety and security to a battleground.

Perhaps the most poignant stress is experienced by the child who watches a beloved brother or sister being drawn into a tight friendship with one of the stepsiblings. Sometimes the twosome even excludes the original partner who is now considered too young or too old, too clinging or too bossy.

One of the irritations which is likely to be overlooked by the remarried couple is the change their alliance has made in each of their children's ordinal position in the group. An oldest brother may suddenly find himself in the middle of the pack, stripped of his seniority and status. A pampered youngest sister may be expected to babysit a toddler and handle unaccustomed chores. An only child may have to adjust to being one of a crowd. Each of these experiences has its own kind of stress which can be exacerbated if it goes unrecognized by the parents.

Living in Two Households. When children live in two different households for part of each year, what happens in one home inevitably affects life in the other (Jacobson 1983). Children report that the best situation is when their step and biological fathers and step and biological mothers get along well together (Rofes 1982). In such cases, they benefit from two complete families which interact harmoniously and which provide them with a rich variety of role models. When relationships between the two households are acrimonious, the children are torn and troubled. Some parents give their youngsters privileges and punishments with an eye to the way in which these events will aggravate the former spouse (Jacobson 1980). Others demand that their children prove their loyalty by bringing home tales of discord from their visits to the second household. Parental battle tactics in which children are used as weapons create a great deal of stress. The strain increases as the depth of a child's love for each family grows.

If the relationship between the two sets of parents is pleasant or at least neutral, children tend to thrive in joint-custody situations. Most say they have little difficulty in accepting that each household has different rules (Luepnitz 1982). And though the first plane or bus trip alone may be stressful, most take travel between households in stride. The key to their adjustment seems to be in the repetition of known events at expected times each year. Children experience the most stress when no specific room or space has been set aside for them in the second home. Because of the large size of many combined families, physical space may be at a premium. Use of bathrooms, sleeping arrangements, and allocation of toys are a few of the many sources of conflict.

On the plus side, multiparent children report their pleasure in having lots of adults who love them and give them presents. Some celebrate holidays twice, once with each family. Some enjoy being grandchildren for the first time in their short lives. Singletons may be delighted to have brothers and sisters at last. For older children, the second home may be a source of support, advice, and understanding when things are not going well in the custodial household (Wald 1981).

Sexual Tensions. Sex in the remarried family is seldom discussed but often disturbing to children. The new couple's strong mutual attraction is sensed and feeds into children's sexual fantasies. Youngsters may be embarrassed and overstimulated by the erotic atmosphere (Wald 1981). In nuclear families there are clear taboos against sexual relations between parents and children and among siblings. In multiparent families the taboos are less clear. Prepubertal boys and girls may imagine the new parent or new stepsibling as a potential sexual partner. And the normal sexual exploration and play that goes on between little boys and girls may be upsetting to parents when it occurs among stepsiblings as compared with biological brothers and sisters.

Stress in the Exosystem

American school systems have not yet acknowledged that multiparent families exist. Record cards in elementary schools throughout the country still list only the names and addresses of one set of parents per child (Ricci 1980).

There is no space for information about noncustodial parents. No item offers an opportunity to indicate that a second family is to be notified of emergencies and informed about academic progress. The most important exosystem institution for children ignores the fact that large numbers live in multiparent families.

Children respond to this attitude with an uncomfortable sense of being different from their peers. A child who becomes ill in school and needs to go home may wonder why the nurse, unable to reach his mother on the telephone, doesn't immediately call his father, stepfather, or stepmother. Why does he get only one report card when he has two sets of parents? Why is only his custodial parent invited to conferences with his teachers?

Textbooks portray children as having either one or two parents. On Mother's or Father's Day, youngsters are expected to make only one card and present (Ricci 1980). When they are asked to bring notices home, multiparent children must decide what should go where.

Stress in the Macrosystem

Western mythology labels stepparents (particularly stepmothers) wicked and pities stepchildren for the shabby way in which they are treated. *Step* is a derogatory term. Newspapers describe a federal budget item which has been dropped in favor of another as a "legislative stepchild." Wald (1981) claims that in our culture "step is less." The message is clear to multiparent youngsters. Even before they meet their father or mother's new spouse, society has forced them to anticipate that he or she will be mean and cruel. The macrosystem doesn't make it easy for children to accept these new adults without prejudice.

Society's expectations are further defined by popular television shows which usually dramatize only the extremes of stepfamily life. The soap operas feature custody battles and explosions of anger between stepparents and children. The evening situation comedies make it seem as though stepfamilies are all perpetually happy and marvelously loving (Einstein 1980; Wald 1981).

Some kinds of multiparent households are simply ignored by society. Children have no guidelines for their behavior in these instances. For example, they may wonder if it is socially acceptable to go and visit Dad's former live-in lover and her children. Do they have to give up this close relationship just because the adults have separated? And how do youngsters introduce their mother's homosexual partner and her children when they bring friends home from school?

Legal Rights of Multiparent Children

Biological parents retain all of their legal rights over and responsibilities to their progeny when they remarry. However, their new spouses have virtually no status in relation to these children in the eyes of the law. Although they live in the same house, these grownups and children are legal strangers to one another. No matter how much a child loves and trusts him, a stepfather, for example, cannot give consent for a medical procedure, even in an emergency. And, if an adult initiates a sexual relationship with a stepchild, some authorities maintain that the act should not be considered incest (Wald 1981).

On an everyday level, the contacts between stepparents and stepchildren can be strained by the fact that the youngster's bills are being paid by his or her biological parent. Some children report that they use this knowledge as an excuse to refuse to accept their stepparent's authority.

In most states the law cannot force stepparents to contribute money for the stepchildren's food, clothing, and shelter unless they have gone through legal adoption procedures. To date, only California, New Jersey, and New York protect stepchildren whose families would otherwise have to go on welfare by requiring stepparents to provide financial support (Kargman 1983). If the remarriage ends in another divorce, stepchildren have no protection unless, on a case-by-case basis, a judge orders a stepparent to provide for them. At the time of the second divorce, children feel completely helpless to influence their own lives, maintain an accustomed standard of living, continue in a school they know and love, and keep contact with cherished stepfamily members.

How Multiparent Children Cope

As their numbers grow, so does knowledge about the stresses affecting multiparent children. Dozens of books are available on the subject. The Stepfamily Association of America, a national society specifically designed for remarried parents, has been functioning actively since 1980. Their goal is to help members learn how to cope with their own and their children's stresses.

Daily newspapers feature articles on how to decorate rooms for part-time sons and daughters. Columnists poke fun at the two-parent youngster who has only one home and is jealous of his multiparent classmates. As more remarried parents become educated to the problems of these youngsters, some of the stresses inherent in this family constellation are likely to fade.

Perhaps most hopeful of all is the fact that these children have so many adults to whom they can turn for help. Werner and Smith (1982) found that those children who received positive feedback and affection from adults in their immediate environment were more likely to be able to deal effectively with stress. In multiparent families such opportunities come with the territory. Tensions in one household can be set aside for a time by visiting the other. Eight grandparents and a multitude of aunts and uncles distanced by geography and age can be objective and wise when a youngster needs them. Thus, while the potential for stress is greatest in multiparent as compared with one- and two-parent homes, so too is the potential for providing solace and opportunities for growth.

Childhood Stress in Communal Living Groups

In contrast to multiparenting, communal parenting produces different kinds of stress for children, yet helps them to cope in many of the same ways. A longitudinal study by the Family Styles Project at the University of California at Los Angeles has begun to delineate some of the effects of communal life on children from birth to six years. These researchers have been able to maintain contact with a sample of more than fifty families domiciled in communes in various parts of California. All of the communities are isolated from mainstream society both geographically and in the value they place on group decision making regarding all phases of family life (Eiduson 1983a).

The sample represents two kinds of communes, one of which espouses a specific religious creed and requires obedience to parental values from their children. The other, humanistic and unstructured, encourages self-expression and self-motivation in their children. Both teach youngsters to cooperate rather than compete, to conform to the larger group's values, and to accept that they are different from outsiders. Children are expected to relate warmly to multiple caretakers and depend less on their biological mothers and fathers as they grow older. Commune parents say their goal is to protect their progeny from the stresses of the traditional middle-class homes of their own childhoods (Alexander and Kornfein 1983).

Sources of Stress

The major stress for children in communes grows out of the unique parent-child relationship typical of this form of living. Community values dictate that all parents treat all children equally. Because any adult in the group can function in the role of parent, children are expected to take orders and accept comforting from everybody. Thus mothers and fathers feel free to take trips away from the commune for two weeks or more, even in their infant's first months. Despite their parents' good intentions, children report that they experience stress when there are too many adults to listen to, when they feel betrayed because their biological mother or father won't stand up for them to other members of the community, and when they experience the pain of separation while their parents are away on trips. The Family Styles Project found that children did less well in school at times when they were experiencing these kinds of stress (Eiduson 1983b). Other childhood tensions in communal settings were apparently minor and had little if any effect on school performance. These included the fact that most commune families lived at the poverty level, provided their youngsters with few toys, and, in humanistic communes, exposed them to displays of adult sexuality (Eiduson 1983b).

Commune children who attend public schools find themselves in a similar situation to multiparent youngsters. Teachers have little understanding of what it is like to grow up in a communal setting. And, of course, school records make no provision for listing a group of adults as parents. Most youngsters are helped to manage this kind of stress by the community's adults who urge them to take pride in being different from the outsiders they meet in school.

How Commune Children Cope

Communes provide children with a rich variety of models of coping strategies. There are caring adults in the home at all times to whom children can turn. The Family Styles Project found that communal families have lower total stress levels than is common in traditional two-parent households. They speculate that because these groups solve their problems by changing their routines and ways of behaving, children become used to continual exposure to new ways of doing things. They experience this as productive rather than stressful (Eiduson 1983b).

Youngsters are also helped to learn to cope with stress by the rest of the children in the community. No other family lifestyle builds such strong ties among unrelated children of both sexes and a wide variety of ages. Commune youngsters develop deep loving relationships with their almost-siblings, who become their dearest friends.

References

Alexander, J., and M. Kornfein. 1983. Changes in family functioning amongst nonconventional families. *American Journal of Orthopsychiatry*, 53:408–417.

Eiduson, B.T. 1983a. Children of the children of the 1960's: An introduction. *American Journal of Orthopsychiatry*, 53:400–407.

————. 1983b. Conflict and stress in nontraditional families: Impact on children. *American Journal of Orthopsychiatry*, 53:426–435.

Einstein, L. 1980. Stepfamily: Chaotic, complex, challenging. *Stepfamily Bulletin*, Fall.

Furstenberg, F. 1983. Divorce and child adjustment. Paper presented at conference, *Current Research in Divorce and Remarriage*. Sixtieth annual meeting of the American Orthopsychiatric Association, April 8, Boston.

Jacobson, D.S. 1980. Stepfamilies. *Children Today*, January–February.

————. 1983. Stepfamily interaction and child adjustment. Paper presented at conference, *Current Research in Divorce and Remarriage*. Sixtieth annual meeting of the American Orthopsychiatric Association, April 8, Boston.

Kargman, M.W. 1983. Stepchild support obligations of stepparents. *Family Relations*, 32:231–238.

Luepnitz, D.A. 1982. *Child custody: A study of families after divorce*. Lexington, Mass.: Lexington Books, D.C. Heath and Company.

Ricci, I. 1980. Divorce, remarriage and the schools. *Stepfamily Bulletin*, Fall.

Rofes, E.E. ed. 1982. *The kids' book of divorce: By, for and about kids*. New York: Vintage Books, a division of Random House.

Wald, E. 1981. *The remarried family: Challenge and promise*. New York: Family Service Association of America.

Warshak, R.A., and J.W. Santrock 1983. The impact of divorce in father-custody and mother-custody homes: The child's perspective. In *Children and divorce*, ed. L.A. Kurdek. San Francisco: Jossey-Bass Inc., Publishers.

Werner, E.E., and R.S. Smith. 1982. *Vulnerable but invincible: A longitudinal study of resilient children and youth*. New York: McGraw-Hill Book Company.

5 Permanent Separation: Death and Adoption

Halfway along the spectrum of childhood stress lie those events which separate children from family members. Every separation brings with it change, pain, and dislocation. Permanent losses may be somewhat less stressful than temporary absences, since they generally require only one major change in lifestyle. Yet, acceptance of a permanent separation takes many months and involves a complex process of what has been called grief-work. When a parent or sibling has been lost, it may be two or more years before grieving is completed.

Children's reactions to separation depend on their ages and stages of cognitive functioning. Only very young infants seem to be unaffected. As early as seven months, most show their distress in ways which resemble adult patterns of mourning (Bowlby 1980). Their responses to separation begin with some form of protest, which may include anxiety, anger, and denial. This is followed by a period of despair, sadness, and depression. At last acceptance occurs and with it a willingness to allow new attachments.

Watching children make their way through these stages of grief is painful for most adults. As a result, many attempt to shield their youngsters by surrounding the facts of death or separation with secrecy. Children in turn realize that their own visible hurt causes discomfort to adults, so they hide their feelings (Lewis and Martin 1983). Grownups are frequently misled in their judgments of the depth of children's misery by the fact that most youngsters can tolerate only short outbursts of grief. Children are easily distracted and thus appear to be done with mourning long before this is actually the case (Bowlby 1980).

A survey of current research concludes that the damaging effects of separation can be modified by two important micro- and exosystem factors. Children who have healthy and happy relationships with their parents before the separation or death occurs apparently enter the stressful situation with a sort of immunization. The years of warmth and caring have taught them effective ways of facing and handling problems. As a result, they cope more easily than other youngsters. It has also been found that children who are given high-quality care by surviving family members during the mourning period, or who are effectively helped by caretakers in foster homes or other exosystem institutions, experience less separation distress. Excellent relationships between youngsters and substitute caregivers can ease stress levels and promote normal development (Garmezy 1983).

Death

Death of a Parent

The majority of children survive a parent's death with only minor emotional scars. If this were not so, "we should expect the development of every child or adolescent who lost a parent to be impaired, which we know is not the case" (Bowlby 1980, 318). However, all children need adult help in order to cope effectively. Experts agree that long-term functioning can be enhanced or damaged by (1) the way in which children learn of a parent's death, (2) whether they take part in some sort of funeral or memorial ritual, and (3) the quality of care they receive in the following weeks and months.

Telling Children about a Parent's Death. If a parent's death occurred in a hospital, his or her children may not learn about it for hours or even days. Surviving parents and other relatives often find it hard to break the news. They may delay or give misleading messages. Being told that Daddy has gone to heaven (unless the family has a deep religious belief in this concept) or is away on a trip may produce fantasies that he will come back. Hearing that Mommy has gone to sleep may produce fear of being put to bed at night. Therapists urge concerned adults to tell children the news as soon as possible; to be clear and direct about what has happened; to express their own sadness and pain; and to give the youngsters sympathy and support in expressing their misery. Grownups should be prepared for changes in the children's behavior. For a time, youngsters are likely to seem more depend-ent and submissive than usual and to deny rather than express their feelings. Some even appear to have suicidal wishes (Berlinsky and Biller 1982).

If children witness a parent being murdered, committing suicide, being killed in an accident or natural disaster, even the best efforts of the surviving relatives may not be sufficient to help them deal with their terror and confu-sion. Short-term therapy for adults and children together may be necessary before healthy coping can begin. Pruett (1979) describes a successful thera-peutic intervention with an elderly couple and their two toddler grandchildren. The little children had watched their father shoot their mother and were then left alone with the body for some hours before neighbors called for help. When a homicide is committed in front of the victim's children, psychologists urge that these youngsters be offered immediate professional counseling.

Attending the Funeral. When children are sent to stay with friends or rela-tives until after the funeral, they are barred from a helpful experience. Child-ren can better understand and face the reality of loss by seeing the coffin or urn, watching the interment, and later visiting the grave to leave flowers and perhaps say a prayer. They gain comfort from attending a memorial service and listening to descriptions of the parent's life and accomplishments. Preparation for these experiences is important. Youngsters need to know in advance what will happen during the ceremony, whether they will see the body, and how to respond to expressions of sympathy (Berlinsky and Biller 1982).

The Quality of Care after a Parent's Death. The quality of care which children receive after a parent's death appears to be crucial to healthy functioning (Garmezy 1983). Youngsters who are supported in mourning at those times when they feel moved to do so are most likely to make their way through grief to acceptance. During this time it may be helpful for an adult to fill in, at least temporarily, for the dead parent. Fathers typically find mother substitutes to work in the household. Mothers have more difficulty in locating suitable adults for the surrogate role (Berlinsky and Biller 1982).

Sometimes the surviving family members cannot cope on their own and need professional help. A combination of two or more of the following behaviors may indicate that additional adult support, counseling, or therapy is needed:

deep and persisting fears that other loved ones will die or that the child himself will die

repeated expressions of wanting to die in order to be with the dead parent

angry and violent outbursts combined with feelings of guilt for the parent's death

attempted role reversal from depending on the surviving adult to taking care of him or her

continual movement, inability to be quiet or to express sad feelings

marked reduction in activity by a formerly very active child

Death of a Sibling

The death of a sibling may be more difficult for children to understand and accept than the loss of a parent. Most believe that only old people die, so a child's demise shakes their faith in their own immortality. The majority seem to be able to cope effectively if they are helped through an appropriate mourning period. However, support is usually less available to them than it is to their parents. When a child dies, institutions and individuals in the exosystem rally to the aid of bereaved adults and often ignore the suffering of younger members of the family. In fact, adults may not recognize that some childish actions are ways of coping with loss. Children's expressions of misery are different from the adult's sadness and tears. Many youngsters will regress to earlier, more infantile behaviors (e.g., bedwetting, loss of speech, demand for bottle feeding). Others will not want to eat, appear dazed, have nightmares, or talk compulsively about death. Some become unusually anxious and timid; others uncharacteristically aggressive and antisocial. All of these behaviors are normal reactons to a sibling's death and may persist for weeks.

Research on the effects of sibling death points to four sources of stress. These include (1) the way in which the child died, (2) parental reactions to the death, (3) parental feelings toward the surviving youngsters, and (4) children's relationships with their siblings prior to and after the loss.

Circumstances of Death. The sudden death of a brother or sister is traumatic for the surviving siblings. Children who witness death experience a depth of horror that may require the services of a therapist. They cannot deny or forget what they have seen. Siblings who have not been present are shielded from some of the anguish. They can have the comfort of occasionally denying reality (Bank and Kahn 1982).

Loss of a sibling by degrees, as in a terminal illness or when death comes several days after an accident, creates an array of stressful situations for survivors. First there is the strain of observing the pain and suffering of the injured youngster. In addition, children lose the companionship and attention of their parents, who spend every waking moment tending to the needs of the dying child. The well siblings are expected to be on their own, independent, and self-sufficient. Compounding these stresses is the guilt most feel when they allow themselves to lead normal lives while a sibling is dying (Bank and Kahn 1982).

A brother or sister's suicide creates its own brand of stress since it leaves questions and self-accusations which can never be answered or assuaged. Two questions, "What could I have done to make my sibling want to live?" and "What did I do to make him want to die?" haunt survivors for the rest of their lives. Equally distressing is the sense of blame that results when a child thinks that his unspoken wish that a sibling didn't exist actually caused the youngster to kill himself (Bank and Kahn 1982).

Children are under the heaviest load of stress when they have been active participants in the incident leading to a sibling's death. These youngsters need expert help in understanding and eventually forgiving themselves. Many are feared by their siblings and parents and never become trusted members of the family again. Similar distrust occurs when families believe that children do not show appropriate grief or are actually glad that a brother or sister has died (Cain, Fast, and Erickson 1979).

Parents' Reactions. The way in which parents respond to a child's death can facilitate or distort the surviving siblings' grief work. No matter how effective they are in supporting their youngsters, however, the death removes the adult's aura of being a secure protector. Youngsters are forced to realize that their parents cannot prevent them from dying. Loss of faith in adult strength increases the existing stress.

Parents have a difficult time in the weeks immediately following a son or daughter's death and most function less adequately than usual. A few become immobilized; mothers unable to give love or attention; fathers erecting a wall between themselves and the outside world and hardly hearing the children when they talk (Cain, Fast, and Erickson 1979). The consequences can be severe when there is no support for the children's grief and no direction for their behavior.

Other parents idealize the dead child and compare the remaining siblings to this unreal portrait. Living sons and daughters are labeled inadequate and their self-confidence erodes. Some cope by refusing to try or deliberately failing at tasks.

Another parental reaction is to overprotect the remaining youngsters. Every step the children take is supervised and all risks are removed from daily routines. These children respond by remaining immature and viewing themselves as vulnerable and the world as dangerous. Their normal development toward independence stops or proceeds at a slow pace.

In some cases, parents unconsciously pressure a remaining child to take on the personality and behavior of the dead one. A father whose son has died may seek to recover his loss by taking his daughter to sports events, teaching her to repair automobiles, and masculinizing her role in the family. These children live with the stress of being two people at once. Many become convinced that their parents would have been more content if they had died in place of their sibling.

A few families impose a rule of silence following a sibling's death. Parents believe that it is best not to talk about the loss so as not to upset the children. The siblings, recognizing their parents' discomfort, also avoid mentioning their brother or sister. Feelings that might have been shared are bottled up and kept under the surface. Children have no opportunity to grieve or to learn to cope with their sadness.

Sibling Relationships. The ability to adapt to the stress of losing a sibling is strongly influenced by the relationship which existed between the children in the years preceding the death. If they were loving and close, yet kept their individual identities, the survivor will probably experience a minimum of stress during the mourning period (Bank and Kahn 1982).

Where the siblings were twins or were so close as to feel that each was part of the other's identity, the death of one partner produces extreme distress for the survivor. These youngsters feel that they have lost a major portion of themselves (Bank and Kahn 1982). They are no longer sure who they are. They must undergo the long process of reconstructing their personalities and finding their own lifestyles. Some come to believe that they will die in the same manner or (if they happen to be the younger of the pair) die at the same age as the sibling.

Brothers and sisters who hated each other or were fiercely competitive prior to their sibling's death seem to experience the most stress. Stored-up anger and guilt are difficult emotions to cope with and these children are seldom successful unless they get help from concerned adults. Their behavior is generally so far removed from what a grownup would consider appropriate mourning that it is not recognized as a way of coping. These children, instead of crying, find ways to cause others to punish them; they think that punishment will relieve their feelings of guilt and let the world know what bad people they believe themselves to be (Bank and Kahn 1982). Some become the victims of accidents or turn aggressive, taunting their teachers and peers and breaking rules. Others fail school subjects in which they had done well previously and develop learning disabilities. When acting out no longer numbs their overwhelming guilt, they become depressed. If help is accepted early enough, they can face their feelings and move on to constructive growth. In too many cases, however, destructive, angry behavior is not recognized as a way of denying sadness and pain, and these children's life stresses increase in spiral fashion.

On the other hand, death in the sibling group can have a positive result for the whole family. Brothers and sisters can be drawn closer together as they work to restructure their roles in relation to one another and to their parents. When older siblings become more nurturing of younger ones, all of the children feel more responsibility for the happiness of the group.

Miscarriage and Stillbirth. The death of an expected brother or sister through miscarriage or stillbirth undoubtedly has some effect on the older siblings, but as yet, there are no research results to guide practitioners. Parental reports are sketchy but indicate that children grieve. An informal survey by Borg and Lasker (1981) suggests that, in addition to sadness, surviving children may feel disappointment and anger that their parents did not keep their promise to produce a baby. Most adults are understandably reluctant to prepare their youngsters for the possibility that a pregnancy may not result in a healthy, living infant. As a result, the actual fact of death may be even more shocking to the children than to the adults.

A typically childlike reaction to miscarriage and stillbirth is one that parents and relatives frequently ignore. This is the child's assumption that if Mom and Dad are so upset at the fact that this baby did not live, then they must be dissatisfied with the youngsters they already have. Self-esteem drops markedly in these cases and may lead to behavior that is difficult to understand unless adults recognize that the cause lies in children's mistaken undervaluation of themselves.

Children's Concepts of Death

Knowing what children believe about death can help adults to understand their behavior in the period following the loss of a parent or sibling. When a three-year-old creeps from his bed every night and runs down the street looking for his dead mother, is he mourning for her? When six-year-old spends an entire afternoon drawing pictures of coffins and graveyards, is he doing some sort of grief work? When a nine-year-old can't wait to go back to school after the funeral so he can tell his classmates how his brother died, is this a denial of grief?

Of course, all are ways in which children cope with their losses. And all follow the youngster's own logic. Most psychologists who deal directly with bereaved children accept the theory that there are three stages to their understanding of death. These roughly parallel Piaget's stages of cognitive development and involve children's ability to grasp the concept that some things cannot be reversed.

Three- to five-year-olds think that dead people live on "under changed circumstances" (Lonetto 1980, 165). The missing person is just that— missing—and youngsters expect him to return. When he stays away, they are hurt and angry at being abandoned. They want to go to heaven to bring the dead person home. Caretakers are asked where dead people's houses are, what they eat, and why they won't be cold if they are buried without hats and coats in winter.

By the time they enter first grade and until about the end of third grade, children conceive of death as a person (Lonetto 1980). Halloween decorations and games portraying death as a skeleton, ghost, or monster, have great appeal and probably serve to reinforce their belief. Children become fascinated by funerals and burial rituals. They talk about what happens to bodies after death. Because death is a person, he can be fought and overcome if one's magic is strong enough. Thus, young and healthy children don't die. Death captures and takes away only those old and sick people who are too weak to conquer him.

At some time during their ninth year, most youngsters begin to grasp the concept that death is the end of life and is not reversible; it is an abstract idea (Lonetto 1980). They realize that they too will die. Despite the television shows which imply that death is clean, quick, and easy, children begin to understand that it may be a painful process.

Helping Children Cope with Death

Many books have been written for adults on how to facilitate children's grief work. There is considerable agreement among authors on techniques which they believe to be helpful. For the most part, these strategies were developed by clinicians and religious counselors working with bereaved youngsters. Their effectiveness has yet to be validated through research studies.

Table 5-1 brings together the suggestions about which there is agreement. All of the authors summarized here caution that any activity be limited to brief sessions repeated only when the child seems ready for more. In table 5-1, the left-hand column describes typical ways in which children try to deal with their grief. Next to each is a synthesis of current recommendations for therapeutic responses (Bank and Kahn 1982; Bowlby 1980; Cain, Fast, and Erickson 1979; Grollman 1976; Jewett 1982; Lewis and Martin 1983; Lonetto 1980; Pruett 1979). Jewett's (1982) book, "Helping Children Cope with Separation and Loss," gives detailed descriptions of many of the helping strategies mentioned in this compilation.

Adoption

It is difficult for most people to conceive of adoption as stressful for children. After all, this is a process by which homeless youngsters become wanted members of healthy, welcoming, usually two-parent families. Because of the careful screening given to prospective adoptive parents by state and private agencies, most have more than adequate incomes. Often the family is a relatively small one and the mother is a highly educated housewife (Bachrach 1983). Indeed, for infants who have never known other parents, adoption creates no ripples at all in the smooth functioning of their daily lives. However, for older children, adoption almost always begins with a sense of

Table 5-1
Strategies for Helping Children Cope with Death

Children's Behaviors	Helpful Adult Responses
Protest Stage	
Apparently not hearing or not understanding the news of the death; acting dazed.	Repeat the news later in the day or the next morning. Answer questions clearly and honestly. Wait for awareness to occur.
Panic and fear of being alone; nightmares.	Maintain usual routines as far as possible. Be sure children know who will take care of them in the coming weeks. At night keep a radio playing or leave a door open so the child can hear sounds of life. Be sure someone is near to comfort the child after a nightmare.
Grabbing the limelight to tell about the death.	Allow this. It won't last long.
Denying that the death has occurred; being unusually active and boisterous to keep from thinking about it.	Accept this behavior. If it persists more than three to six months, consult a therapist (Jewett 1982).
Grief Stage	
Sadness and tears, yearning, acute loneliness.	Share adult sadness and tears with children. Support crying; join in yearning. Hold, cuddle, touch. Review pleasant and unpleasant memories of the dead person. Together make a memory book of photos captioned by the child. Collect home movies, videotapes, and tape recordings for the memory file.
Regression to earlier, more infantile behavior.	Accept and facilitate (e.g., if wanted, give a toddler a bottle), yet support attempts to regain mature skills.
Searching for the dead person.	Allow this to continue until the child feels he or she has made a thorough search. Help child to talk about repeated disappointments.
Difficulty in school, inability to concentrate, development of learning disability.	School problems may last as long as two years. Teachers can work with the class around death issues; have the school counselor work regularly with the child on personal problems so he or she can concentrate during class. Help children keep at their studies but do not allow this to cut into their playtime.
Anger and guilt. Anger may be misplaced and directed toward caretaker, siblings, adults in the exosystem.	Accept anger, understanding that it is misplaced. Empathize with and respect feelings. Reassure that hurting is part of grieving and eventually will subside. Find physical outlets for children's rage. Put aside adult activities when possible to emphasize the value of conversations about guilty or angry feelings. Encourage drawing, writing, and playing out feelings. Where possible, meet periodically with the siblings as a group to explore feelings of guilt and anger and work out solutions to common problems with their new living situation.

Table 5-1 (continued)

Hopelessness and despair.	Validate such feelings as legitimate and painful. Reassure child they are temporary. Use books and stories to show how others coped with death. Reading fairy tales where a child conquers adversity is a way to help restore meaning and hope (Bettelheim 1975).
Acceptance Stage	
Acceptance of loss; seeking closer bonds with new caretaker; strengthening relationships with siblings.	Allow memory of dead person to be a part of children's present lives by remembering anniversaries, recalling feelings.

loss and a period of mourning. The amount and kind of stress experienced depends in large part on the type of legal agreement the parents choose. The law in most states offers a choice of traditional (closed) or open adoption.

Traditional Adoption

Traditional adoption attempts to give children the same feelings they would have if they were born into the new family. They have no past other than the one they share with their adoptive parents. To insure that this happens, all court and agency records are sealed and neither set of parents knows the other's identity. Theoretically, under these circumstances, children and parents have a good chance of making deep and permanent commitments to one another. Adoptive mothers and fathers are trained to expect a mourning period and to help their youngsters complete the grieving process.

Borgman (1982) identifies a number of sources of stress in traditional adoption. These generally affect youngsters who are three or more years old and who can remember their birth parents, foster home(s), friends, relatives, teachers, and neighbors. For these children there is major stress in cutting all of these important ties. Many measure their self-worth by the way they are treated by the significant adults in their lives. When they lose these people, they lose their sense of identity too.

Another stress grows out of the memories children manufacture about their birth and foster parents. Some mistakenly remember these mothers and fathers as saints or as monsters. Either fantasy inhibits the bond with the new family. Previously abused or neglected children often end up with low self-esteem when they believe that their own bad behavior caused them to be taken away from their "real" parents (Borgman 1982).

In closed adoption situations, recent studies have found that older children are likely to persist in keeping contact with adults and peers who were important to them in the past, even when this is forbidden. Knowing that they are breaking the rules and not being honest with their adoptive parents is an additional source of stress (Borgman 1982).

Open Adoption

In contrast to the traditional emphasis on secrecy, open adoption procedures aim to build and support constructive relationships among children and both sets of parents. Long before this form of adoption became the fashionable alternative for educated couples, informal open adoptions occurred when-ever parents voluntarily asked grandparents or other family members to raise their children. In legal open adoptions, birth and adoptive parents maintain regular contact. Sometimes the birth mother and father help to choose the adoptive family.

Under this form of adoption, children have little mourning to do. When they gain a new family they do not lose the old one. They have the security of knowing that their adoptive mother and father accept them as they are, including the parents who gave them up for adoption. A number of researchers have found that regular contact helps children to picture their birth parents realistically as neither too wonderful nor too awful (Borgman 1982). They come to understand why they were placed for adoption, and this increases self-esteem.

The stresses in open adoption come from the contrasts which children experience between their new and old family values. At the same time, there is the advantage of having a large number of relatives to turn to for help and advice.

Adoption of Sibling Groups

Traditional adoption procedures can create severe stress if all members of a sibling group are not accepted by one couple. When each is sent to a separate home, children report that the pain is similar to experiencing a sibling's death. Yet it is common practice for social agencies to separate sibling groups. Often the reasons are valid: adoptive parents cannot be found who are willing to take all the children, foster parents want to adopt only the youngster they already love, or one of the children is handicapped and needs a special living situation (Depp 1983). In open adoption, contact is main-tained among the siblings, even when they must be placed in homes some distance from one another. This practice alleviates some of the grief, but creates more stress than would occur if the group were kept together.

Adoption is a stressful experience, even for brothers and sisters placed together. Besides grieving for their lost parents or foster home(s), they feel insecure with their new living arrangements. One strategy that adoption workers know well occurs when the siblings gang up against the adoptive parents. Other children form themselves into a tight and separate family with an older child acting as their pseudoparent. This may last for many months until all feel secure enough to accept their new mother and father (Depp 1983). As a result, many couples seek counseling or therapy for one or more of the youngsters or for the whole family during the early stages of a sibling group adoption.

Helping Children Cope with Adoption

Children over the age of three need help in grieving for the significant people from their former lives who will become more peripheral as the years go by. The techniques advocated for helping children cope with death are also used by adoption workers. Jewett (1982) suggests that adults help youngsters say goodbye to the old relationships in symbolic ways which fill the same function as funerals and memorial services.

Anniversaries of important events in children's earlier lives may bring unconscious responses that youngsters find stressful. It seems helpful for adults to anticipate and plan appropriate activities with the children to remember these dates and to talk about wishes for what might have been. Most important of all, the new home needs to welcome the memories of the old one(s), yet maintain itself as a distinct and different place with distinct and different relationships (Jewett 1982).

References

Bachrach, C.A. 1983. Children in families: Characteristics of biological, step-, and adopted children. *Journal of Marriage and the Family*, 45:171–179.

Bank, S.P., and M.D. Kahn. 1982. *The sibling bond*. New York: Basic Books, Inc., Publishers.

Berlinsky, E.B., and H.B. Biller. 1982. *Parental death and psychological development*. Lexington, Mass.: Lexington Books, D.C. Heath and Company.

Bettelheim, B. 1975. Reflections: The uses of enchantment. *The New Yorker*, December 8.

Borg, S., and J. Lasker. 1981. *When pregnancy fails: Families coping with miscarriage, stillbirth, and infant death*. Boston: Beacon Press.

Borgman, R. 1982. The consequences of open and closed adoption for older children *Child Welfare*, 61:217–226.

Bowlby, J. 1980. *Attachment and loss, Volume III, Loss: Sadness and depression.* New York: Basic Books, Inc., Publishers.

Cain, A.C., I. Fast, and M.E. Erickson. 1979. Children's disturbed reactions to the death of a sibling. In *Human adaptation: Coping with life crises*, ed. R.H. Moos. Lexington, Mass.: D.C. Heath and Company.

Depp, C.H. 1983. Placing siblings together. *Children Today*, March–April.

Garmezy, N. 1983. Stressors of childhood. In *Stress, coping, and development in children*, ed. N. Garmezy and M. Rutter. New York: McGraw–Hill Book Company.

Grollman, E.A. 1976. *Talking about death: A dialogue between parent and child.* Boston: Beacon Press.

Jewett, C.L. 1982. *Helping children cope with separation and loss.* Harvard, Mass.: The Harvard Common Press.

Lewis, S., and J.E. Martin. 1983. Children and loss: A preventive educational multimedia program for parents and teachers. Paper presented at conference, *Current research in divorce and remarriage.* Sixtieth annual meeting of the American Orthopsychiatric Association, April 8, Boston.

Lonetto, R. 1980. *Children's conceptions of death.* New York: Springer Publishing Company.

Proch, K. 1982. Differences between foster care and adoption: Perceptions of adopted foster children and adoptive foster parents. *Child Welfare*, 61:259–268.

Pruett, K.D. 1979. Home treatment for two infants who witnessed their mother's murder. *Journal of the American Academy of Child Psychiatry*, 18:647–657.

Rutter, M. 1983. Stress, coping and development: Some issues and some questions. In *Stress, coping, and development in children*, ed. N. Garmezy and M. Rutter. New York: McGraw–Hill Book Company.

Sorich, C.J., and R. Siebert. 1982. Toward humanizing adoption. *Child Welfare*, 61:207–216.

6

Temporary Separation

In the midrange of the spectrum of stresses, military service, hospitalization, foster care, and incarceration all involve temporary separation of children and parents. Illness, physical or mental handicaps, and foster placement keep siblings apart temporarily. Research on the effects of these separations indicates that when the reason is known and the length can be accurately estimated, there is minimal stress for children. But the effects can be severe when children are uncertain as to why parents or siblings have left and when they will see them again. Anger at being abandoned and fear that loved ones will not return are typical responses. Hunter and Hickman (1981) cite studies to show that children whose soldier fathers are prisoners of war (i.e., who know the location of the prison camp and expect eventual repatriation) suffer less stress than youngsters whose fathers are missing in action.

Additional stress occurs when the parent or sibling returns to the family. After the first moments of joy, pent-up anxieties are triggered, making re-entry awkward and painful. In addition, while the family member has been absent the remaining children have taken on different roles and developed new interests and habits. Their behavior is no longer familiar to the one who is returning. If he or she demands that everything go back to the way it was, the necessary role and behavior flip-flops may require more flexibility than some children can muster (Hunter and Hickman 1981).

When separations occur repeatedly, the resulting stress may be left unresolved for years. Each reunion brings renewed hope, a period of satisfaction, and then another wrench as the relationship is pulled apart. Some children cope with the tension by becoming unusually manic and aggressive; others become withdrawn, depressed, and tearful. Some express hostility toward family members by regressing or by doing poorly in school.

Separation from Parents

Children seem to experience psychological separation more deeply than they do physical distance from parents. They can remain emotionally connected to a father who is three thousand miles away if there are frequent exchanges of telephone calls, letters, photographs, and tapes. Conversely, they can feel estranged from a noncommunicative mother who is staying with a sick relative across town. Caretakers other than parents can also be missed desperately if children have lived with and grown to care about these adults.

Separations due to military service, hospitalization, placing children in foster care, or a parent's incarceration all produce similar stresses for children. However, in addition, each has its unique problems for which youngsters must evolve special adaptive strategies.

Military Service

The armed services have funded several studies to explore the effects of father absence on military families. The results place a heavy burden on the homebound spouse. Women who can keep their households running smoothly, not give in to loneliness, and maintain their husbands in the father role even though they are absent, have been found to produce children who adjust successfully. To quote the wife of a Marine who apparently mastered the necessary coping skills, "He is missed, but his absence is accepted, as it is known that's our way of life" (Hillenbrand 1976, 453). Today more military wives work full-time than was true in the 1970s when that statement was written. It is likely that in the 1980s fewer children have mothers who can provide them with home lives stable enough to offset the stress of frequent tour-of-duty separations.

Some sources of stress for military youngsters are outlined in table 6-1. It should be noted that elementary school children can be expected to have more difficulty in coping with father absence than those who are under the age of five (Hunter and Hickman 1981). Next to each source of stress listed in table 6-1 are suggested techniques for helping children to cope. While the effectiveness of these strategies is generally accepted by professionals who work with military families (Hunter and Hickman 1981; Lexier 1981), none has been put to the test of controlled research.

Hospitalization

A parent's hospitalization always disturbs children's daily routines, changes accustomed roles, and gives rise to fears about the unknown. Disruption of routines produces stress, especially when youngsters must adjust to new caretakers. Children have to learn to cope with alterations in the patient's personality and accept the well parent's preoccupation with the sick one. Not knowing what is going on brings more tension. Recent research on the six- to ten-year-old progeny of cancer patients finds numerous cases of regression among those who are not told that a parent is sick. Youngsters who know about the disease and its treatment maintain an even developmental level (National Cancer Institute 1980).

Table 6-1
Suggested Ways to Help Military Dependents Cope with Separation

Source of Stress	Ways to Help Children Cope
Separation anticipated with fear and sadness.	Accept and discuss feelings.
Emotional contact with parent is lost.	Phone calls, letters directed from father especially to children. Mother can encourage children to talk or write to father about their feelings. Keep photos of father in children's rooms.
Belief that father has deliberately abandoned children.	Accept anger as an expression of love and need for contact. Explain reason for separation and likely duration.
Fear engendered by mother's anxieties about father's absence.	Counseling or therapy may be needed for mother and children together.
School viewed as unimportant while father is away.	Father can schedule predeployment conferences with teachers; track children's progress through letters; request mailed reports from teachers.
Difficulty accepting shift in authority from father to mother and back.	"Change of command" ceremonies on leave-taking and return. Discussion with children about rules prior to, during separation and after reunion. Maintaining same family rules at all times.
Resentment of father's inability to recognize and accept change and growth in children.	Prepare for father's return by sending Dad descriptions of children's new accomplishments, responsibilities they now take at home, photos of more grown-up appearance.
Disappointment that relationship with father doesn't return to normal immediately on his return.	Whole family needs to know that it may take them six weeks or more to readjust.

Physical Illness. The three stages in coping with a parent's hospitalization include the weeks of failing health, the period of hospitalization, and the return home for convalescence. Prior to the separation (or between one hospital stay and the next) children are frightened by changes in the adult's behavior, appearance, and ability to relate. They wonder how long he or she will be away and who will take care of them. They are concerned about their own chances of contracting the illness and whether they were somehow the cause.

While the parent is hospitalized, children are likely to feel that they are different from their schoolmates. They are disturbed by necessary changes in daily routines and worried about whether the family will survive this period. When the severity of the illness results in temporary personality change, youngsters wonder if the parent will ever be his or her familiar self again. If relatives blame the doctors and hospital staff for errors of judgment, children lose faith in the ability of medical personnel to heal the patient.

When at last Mom or Dad returns from the hospital, there is an additional period of adaptation. Children are expected to take over household chores, curtail after-school activities, and accept their convalescing parent's need for help and care.

Practitioners who work with the families of cancer, kidney, and other chronic disease patients have evolved strategies for helping children to cope. None have been empirically tested, but at least one set of techniques (Cain and Staver 1976) has been based on a framework postulated by White in the early 1970s. According to White, the process of adapting constructively to stress involves three steps: (1) gathering information about the situation, (2) restoring the organism's internal sense of balance, and (3) initiating action to bring the stressful environment under control, thus allowing a sense of autonomy and efficacy (White 1974).

Table 6–2 summarizes, among others, the suggestions presented by Cain and Staver (1976) for helping children to cope with parental illness and hospitalization.

Mental Illness. The use of psychoactive drugs in the treatment of mental illness has reduced hospital stays from an average of six months in the 1950s to less than three weeks at present. Currently, children of mentally ill parents experience only a brief separation and usually can remain in their own

Table 6–2
Strategies for Helping Children Cope with Parental Hospitalization

Source of Stress	Ways to Help Children Cope
Child lacks information about where parent is, what is happening, how long he or she will be away.	Explain disease in terms child can understand; where parent is and how long he or she will be there; arrange visits if possible. Tell child who will care for him or her and discuss needed changes in routines.
Child feels internally unbalanced, anxious, preoccupied.	Maintain daily contact between child and parent through telephone calls, letters, reports. Put photo of child at parent's bedside and photo of parent in child's room. Keep routines as normal as possible. Encourage well parent to take respite time to engage in recreational activities with children. Support child's hope and belief that family will survive. In school, keep child up to usual academic and behavior standards; maintain normal routines.
Child feels helpless and dependent.	Encourage child to think of ways to help the sick parent; make gifts; assist with nursing care.

homes with the well parent. In many cases, the latter is allowed time off from the job in order to meet increased home responsibilities while the spouse is hospitalized. The whole family is able to maintain contact because recent modernization of regulations in many institutions allow youngsters to visit mentally ill patients (Clausen 1979).

Youngsters experience considerable stress in the days immediately prior to a parent's hospitalization when they witness hallucinatory and other bizarre behavior. The stress can be lessened if the well parent talks honestly with the children about the illness, describes the symptoms they can expect, the kinds of words and actions that are likely to set off further upsets, and explains when to call for help. Parents increase the tension when they attempt to keep their youngsters in line by threatening that their misbehavior will send the patient back to the hospital. In this onset stage, children may be neglected or abused by the mentally ill parent.

In contrast, the weeks when Mom or Dad is in the hospital may be considerably less stressful. This is especially true when successive visits give evidence that he or she is feeling better and becoming more lucid. While the parent is missed, everyone is also grateful for a period of calm and a chance for tempers to cool down.

Researchers agree that the most difficult time for the family is the reentry period. Even today, parents are given little if any guidance by hospital staff on ways to help their children cope with the reunion (Clausen 1979). Often there has not been enough time for youngsters to adjust to the idea that the ill parent will be different, that he or she will not again inflict pain and embarrassment. Their worst fears are realized when the patient is sent home still symptomatic or so heavily drugged that he or she cannot respond. Children report being uneasy about the drugs that have been prescribed for their parents. They wonder if all personality improvements will disappear when the drugs are stopped. They worry about another separation. In many cases, the patient is rehospitalized one or more times before the child reaches adolescence.

Clausen (1979) finds that mentally ill fathers tend to hold jobs despite periods of hospitalization and to do their acting out when their children are not present. While fathers are in the hospital, well mothers live at home and give their youngsters comfort and support. On the other hand, children's lives are deeply disrupted when their mothers are institutionalized. Often youngsters are sent to live with relatives during that period. On her return, they are expected to take over household responsibilities for a mother who may be uncommunicative and emotionally distant. The children find it difficult to accept their well father's diminished presence at home. Husbands of mentally ill patients find many ways to stay away from their families by attending meetings, going to church, or holding down extra jobs. This partial separation compounds the stress for the children, who receive little parenting from either adult (Clausen 1979).

In a series of interviews with the healthy spouses and children of mental patients, Sturges (1978) collected data which suggest that youngsters typically choose from among eight roles in seeking to cope with a mentally ill parent. Sturges maintains that these roles help the whole family to adapt to the repeated separation-reunion experiences. She finds that children often play more than one role at a time or enact several in quick succession. Her descriptions of these strategies makes it clear that each helps the child to cope but at the same time contains the seeds of self-destruction. Table 6–3

Table 6–3
Strategies Children Use in Coping with Mentally Ill Parents

Healthy Aspects	Self-destructive Aspects
Caretaker Takes care of the ill parent; "mothers" the household; defends against own feelings of helplessness.	Doesn't have time to be a child. Doesn't face own anger at and resentment of the patient.
Baby Becomes infantile, whines, clings, allowing self to be dependent; gives other family members a chance to take care of someone who can respond to them.	If continued over time, child doesn't grow toward independent functioning.
Mourner Openly grieves for the temporarily lost parent; helps family express sad feelings.	Continued mourning may develop into chronic depression.
Patient Develops psychosomatic illness; gives family another focus for its attention besides mentally ill parent.	Child may learn to use this as a regular way of getting attention.
Escapee Avoids having to face home problems.	Stays away from home; won't visit patient in hospital; uses overactivity to keep from facing own fears and concerns.
Recluse Defends against own feelings of shame and stigma.	Withdraws and becomes a lonely isolate. Doesn't face own feelings about the patient.
Good Child Does well in school; helps at home; succeeds in almost everything; gives family joy and pride.	Suppresses own feelings about the patient and separation-reunion pattern.
Bad Child Becomes the family scapegoat so they can be angry at him or her instead of the patient.	Behavior is angry, hostile, and defiant and gets child into trouble with authorities in school and community.

uses Sturges' labels for each role and summarizes her descriptions, separating each into its healthy and potentially self-destructive components.

All indications point to the need for outside help for children whose parents are hospitalized from time to time for mental illness. Concerned professionals can start by ascertaining how much the children know about their parent's condition and supplying needed information. Youngsters usually have questions they are afraid to ask about the effects of medication, how long it will be continued, and when (or if) a parent is likely to recover sufficiently to do without pills. They also need help in facing and understanding their own feelings of anger, resentment, and disappointment that they have a parent who doesn't approach the ideal they see on television and read about in books. Finally, they need to learn ways to cope with the patient's demands and still maintain their own individuality and zest for life. The summary of healthy and self-destructive aspects of children's coping styles in table 6-3 suggests behaviors which practictioners can support and others which children may need to give up within a relatively short time.

When Children are Hospitalized

A great deal of attention has been paid to the stress children feel when they are hospitalized. Modern pediatric departments almost uniformly offer educational services to help them to cope. Parents are asked to bring their children to the hospital a day or two before admission so children can see where they will sleep, what they will eat, where the bathrooms are, and learn about the surgery or other care they will receive. Parents report that these programs are helpful in reducing tension, but that they do not eliminate it. Being in a hospital is still equated with being abandoned by loved ones. Children are sure that the pain they feel during medical procedures is punishment for being naughty at home, and they imagine that what is happening to the child in the next bed will also happen to them (Mack 1979).

If they will be absent from school for any length of time, that too is a source of worry. Youngsters' sense of who they are, their worth, skills, and personalities, are closely bound up with their experiences in the classroom. They fear that they will fall so far behind that they will be forced to take lower positions in the academic and social rankings of peers and teachers.

Children with chronic conditions which mandate repeated hospitalization generally respond with one of two nearly opposite points of view. Either they welcome the return to a place where they feel secure, or they fear the hospital and pretend to feel well in order to avoid a return.

There are literally hundreds of books for children and parents which suggest ways to help youngsters cope with the stress of hospitalization. The children's television program, "Mr. Rogers Neighborhood," has addressed the subject several times and has produced a pamphlet for parents.

Table 6–4 lists stresses which have been identified in children prior to, during, and after a hospital stay. Next to each is a brief summary of suggested techniques for helping them cope. Practitioners maintain that these strategies are useful, but as yet, none has been systematically tested. There is general agreement that preparation for a hospital stay probably should begin only a few days in advance so that there is not a long period of anticipatory tension (Mack 1979).

Foster Care

Of all the children under the age of fourteen in the United States today, 1,322,000 are separated from both of their parents. Most of these youngsters live with their grandparents or other relatives, but there are 92,000 children who make their homes with adults who are not related to them. More than 38,000 children age five years and younger are in this category (Bureau of the Census 1982). The census does not count the number of American children who are in foster care, but estimates by the Children's Defense Fund (1978) range from 500,000 to 750,000.

In the 1970s the plight of foster children came under the scrutiny of Congress. Concerned citizens complained that foster children were being shunted from one home to another and kept in care year after year, often hundreds of miles away from their families. Cases were lost and children were forgotten by social agencies. There were no consistent policies regulating foster home quality or mandating efforts to reunite youngsters with their mothers and fathers. As a result, Congress enacted Public Law 96–272, the foster care reform bill. Through various financial incentives, states are now encouraged to keep accurate records of placements, to find homes as close as possible to the children's families, to review each case twice a year, and to try to return children promptly to their parents.

Children are sent to foster placements when the state deems this necessary for their protection; for example, their parents are "too poor, too sick, or too inadequate to bring up children" (Children's Defense Fund 1978, 1), or they have repeatedly been abusive or neglectful. In some cases a parent is in jail, the children have severe behavior problems, or they are so severely retarded or mentally ill that they need supervision from adults with specialized training. Older children, unable to get along with their families, may request foster placement. Probably the greatest stress exists for children who have been abandoned and are found living on the streets or in empty apartments. In this country the number of "throw away" children is small but reported to be growing. In other nations they number in the millions. In

Table 6–4
Ways to Help Children Cope with Hospitalization

Source of Stress	Ways to Help Children Cope
Prior to Hospitalization	
Child lacks information; fears he or she is being hospitalized as punishment for naughty behavior.	Assure this is not punishment; child did nothing wrong. Explain why he or she is going to the hospital and what will happen there. Together make a list of child's questions and be sure all are answered by parent or doctor.
Child fears unknown; worries he or she may never return home.	Visit hospital in advance and talk about it, giving child a day or two to play out what it will be like. Have child help pack bag; take along favorite toy, photos of family. Together, prepare child's room for his or her return as reassurance.
Child remembers previous unhappy separations from parents.	Discuss memories and explain again the need for hospitalization. Make no promises that this separation will be easier.
During Hospitalization	
Child is afraid of pain (needles, surgery, etc.).	Find out what child imagines will happen; give accurate information at child's level of understanding. Accept fears and tears. Affirm that some procedures will hurt. Assure that staff will try to keep pain as brief as possible. Where appropriate, child may be taught relaxation and self-hypnosis techniques to gain control of pain.
Child feels abandoned when parents have to leave.	Make sure child and staff know when parents will leave, when they will return, and why they have to leave. Accept sadness, tears, distress at leave-taking. *Note: Parents of infants and young children have the legal right to stay with their youngsters day and night.*
Child feels confined when not allowed to get out of bed and explore.	Ask why the child thinks he or she is being confined to bed; explain again.
Child feels out of contact with schoolmates, siblings.	Encourage teachers, classmates, siblings, to write cards; visit if feasible.
Convalescence at Home	
Child feels cheated that he or she can't go back to usual activities immediately.	Explain that the child is not well yet but will feel a little better each day.
Home feels unfamiliar and child copes by testing behavior rules, clinging, regressing, demanding attention.	Prepare family for child's reentry, testing, and regression. Discuss with child and family the need for slow readjustment and decide which rules may be temporarily "relaxed."

Brazil for example, there were twenty-five million abandoned youngsters living on the streets of the larger cities in 1981 (Getz 1981).

Foster placement is, by definition, a temporary arrangement in which children are given board and care in return for a fee. Some states will not pay these fees to a child's relatives. Loving grandparents, aunts, and uncles who want the children but who are too poor to feed and clothe them, are out of luck. The state chooses and pays strangers to provide foster homes instead. Clearly, love is not meant to be a part of the bargain. When it develops between foster parents and children, it is sometimes discouraged by the overseeing social agency under the assumption that emotional involvements cause pain when children are returned to their birth parents (Goldstein, Freud, and Solnit 1979). Nonetheless, children report that the best foster experiences occur when they grow to love and respect their surrogate parents.

The Process of Uprooting. Children placed in foster care are like plants being uprooted; they are dug up, transported, and put down again in new places. No matter how carefully the transplanting is done or how much better the supply of nutrients and sunshine in the new location, the move is always a shock to the organism. We do not know what effect such uprooting has on infants because children uniformly report that they cannot remember any other home if the placement was made before they were three years old. Youngsters preschool age or older when first placed describe a variety of stresses on entry into foster care. Most say their first feelings were of grief and sadness. This appears to be true no matter how poorly they were treated at home. Separation from their parents without knowing when they will see them again, and often without knowing why they are being taken away, is traumatic. Typically children do not see the foster home or parents until they are brought to the door by a social worker. They fear the unknown adults. They worry that foster fathers will hit them. Some cry or sit immobilized for hours. Few remember positive feelings until the end of the second week of placement (Allison and Johnson 1981).

The sense of loss in the first weeks extends not only to parents and siblings but to all the people to whom they were attached (i.e., relatives, friends, neighbors, teachers, religious leaders). Children are completely without reference points in the new home. They don't know the neighborhood, the stores, the mores of their age-mates in the area or in the new school. They have lost all of the old markers which helped to establish their feelings of security and self-worth. In the foster home they have to learn a whole new set of routines; how to avoid kinds of punishment they may never have experienced before; how to build relationships with people with whom they did not choose to live. There is some evidence that the process of adjustment becomes more difficult as children get older. One youngster's advice to others on coping with those first weeks in foster care is poignant. "Just pretend that your foster parents are your real parents, and everything will come out fine" (Gil and Bogart 1982, 8).

Moving into foster care with relatives rather than strangers may be somewhat easier for children, but even in these cases there is a deep sense of loss compounded by fear of the change from familiar to less well-known surroundings.

Perhaps the most difficult concept for young children to understand is why they have been uprooted. Many think that their own misbehavior was the cause. Others answer the question with a simple, "I don't know" (Gil and Bogart 1982). Middle-aged or latency youngsters generally are aware that the situation was so bad at home that they had to be taken away from their parents. They talk frankly of being unwanted, unable to get along with their parents, abandoned, abused; they speak of their parents being desperately poor, in jail, or habitually drunk (Allison and Johnson 1981). A few of these children sense and resent their powerlessness. They accept the fact that they cannot control their parents' behavior or improve life at home. But when they have no say in choosing a foster placement, they are acutely aware of being helpless. They may lie, steal, or run away to gain a measure of control or turn to drugs and alcohol in order to feel more powerful, at least for a few hours (Irving 1979).

Living in a Foster Home. Once the initial phase of adjustment is past, children face the prospect of building a relationship with their foster parents. There are a number of reasons why this is not an easy process. By the time they come into care, many youngsters have ambivalent attitudes toward adults. Most have extremely strong yearnings to be taken care of and at the same time equally strong distrust of grownups. As a result, when foster parents cannot meet their unrealistic expectations, youngsters become inappropriately angry and hurt. What the adults experience are a bewildering succession of swings from clinging to aggression and back again (Stein and Derdeyn 1980).

A second factor inhibiting smooth relationships in foster placement is the impermanency of the arrangement. Children expect to go home again. They keep hoping that home will be better than before and nicer than their present placement. They have little incentive to accept and adjust to the foster family.

Then too, older children know that their caretakers are being paid to look after them. They find it hard to accept that any affection shown them is genuine and not simply part of the package the social agency purchased.

When they go to school, foster children feel they are unfairly teased by peers and that the staff treats them differently from other youngsters. They resent being objects of pity and subjected to insensitive questioning by teachers. They find it demeaning to be given good treatment just because they are in foster care. Sometimes they use this as an excuse for doing poorly in their studies. Older children contend that only those open-minded classmates who are willing to admit that their own parents sometimes let them down can understand and sympathize (Allison and Johnson 1981).

Unrecognized and untreated health problems increase stress levels for foster children. Schor (1982) studied the records of foster children in

Baltimore and found these youngsters to be less healthy than average. He speculates that medical care may be postponed because it is expected that children will be returning home soon. Instead, a second or third foster placement may intervene before corrective measures are taken. He reports that chronic health problems like eczema, allergies, and asthma are common among foster children in his city. In addition, needed eyeglasses are not procured, regular visits to dentists are not scheduled, and immunizations against childhood diseases are not given.

There is stress too in the conflicts which children perceive among the adults who are responsible for them. There is tension when natural parents disagree with social workers who disagree with foster couples, and all have a hand in managing the children's lives. Youngsters suspect that social workers don't much care what happens to them; they feel that they are cases, not individuals, in the eyes of the professionals. They resent it when their own wishes are not solicited before changes are made; when they have to have a letter of permission before they can visit their birth parents; when social workers insist on seeing every note that teachers send to foster families (Allison and Johnson 1981).

Finally, there is the utter misery of going home and finding that not enough has changed to make the situation viable. Hundreds of children make the decision each year that they will be better off living in foster care or in group homes rather than with their parents. It is heartbreaking for children to have to acknowledge that their parents will never be able to give them the unconditional love and care that is assumed to be every child's birthright. However, once they have made this decision, the situation seems to improve. A study by Fein and her associates (1983) found that children who had returned to their biological homes at least once and then had gone back to foster care showed better home, school, and emotional adjustment than youngsters who had never been sent back to live with their birth parents.

Helping Foster Children Cope. Fein and her colleagues (1983) report data which demonstrate that youngsters placed in foster care with relatives adjust better than children who are placed in other kinds of temporary homes. She suggests that social workers give relatives first consideration when they choose foster settings. Her findings show that relatives can help children "maintain their sense of family identity, continuity, and human connectedness" (Fein et al. 1983, 552).

Another strategy that is recommended for helping children make the best use of their foster care experience is the construction of a life-story book. According to Aust (1981), this technique has been used successfully for many years. Working together, adult and child fill an album with photos, announcements, greeting cards, documents, and written descriptions of memories of each of his or her previous homes. Movies, videotapes, and audio recordings can be included. The purpose of the compilation is to "change the child's fantasies, distortions, and self-blame into a realistic understanding and acceptance of his and his parents' situation" (Aust 1981, 536).

Several of the stresses experienced by foster children can best be addressed by school personnel. Many youngsters need help in developing their academic and social skills. When these children learn how to succeed academically, make friends, and get along well on the playground, they gain a kind of strength that will stay with them regardless of their home situation. In the process, they also discover that they have a measure of control over what happens to them, at least in school, and no longer feel powerless (Irving 1979). Teachers who respect this need for skill development and who are adept at encouraging social growth in their classrooms can be of real help to foster children.

Incarceration of a Parent

Today there are large numbers of children who are forced to live apart from their parents for varying periods of time, yet who remain unacknowledged by the media and by all but a fraction of the country's child protection agencies. These are children whose parents are in jail. On an average day, conservative estimates put the number of youngsters whose mothers are imprisoned at twenty-one thousand (McGowan and Blumenthal 1978). Probably twenty times that number have incarcerated fathers (Rosenkrantz and Joshua 1982).

Unlike other causes of separation from parents, this one brings children no sympathy from significant people in the exosystem. Even close relatives are reluctant to be identified with criminal behavior and so keep their distance. Children become the innocent victims and pay a steep price for being born to men and women who are convicted and jailed.

Large numbers of children forced by circumstances to live apart from incarcerated parents adopt coping strategies which are self-destructive. Fritsch and Burkhead (1981) queried prisoners in a minimum security prison in Lexington, Kentucky, about their children's adjustment to their absence. Jailed fathers reported that their children had become hostile and aggressive; the children acted out by using drugs and alcohol, were truant, and misbehaved in school. Incarcerated mothers observed that their youngsters had become more withdrawn than before the arrest, cried a lot, had nightmares, feared school, were doing poorly in their studies, and had regressed to earlier behavior patterns. These conclusions are based on parent reports rather than on direct observation of children, thus the differential effects for father and mother absence may be a function of prisoner perceptions. However, regardless of the sex of the parent, it is apparent that children cope by using avoidance mechanisms: denial, regression, withdrawal, and impulsive acting out. Few youngsters receive help in learning ways of adapting which are more conducive to healthy functioning. From the day a parent is arrested to the day he or she is released from jail, children undergo a series of major stresses, most of which they cope with entirely on their own.

Arrest. The first traumatic separation occurs when a mother or father is arrested. Parents picked up by the police away from home are seldom given an opportunity to spend even a few minutes holding and comforting their children. With limited phone privileges, they usually cannot call as many relatives or friends as is necessary to ensure that their children are cared for by people they know and love. If the arrest occurs at home, it is typical for police, sometimes with guns drawn, to remove the suspect while the youngsters watch, without allowing time to make temporary care arrangements or to say goodbye (McGowan and Blumenthal 1978; Stanton 1980). When children live in two-parent families, the remaining parent is their source of support and solace. However, in single-parent situations where a mother is arrested, her children are particularly vulnerable and alone. Their loss is sudden and often terrifying.

Pretrial Period. Suspects may be detained overnight or held for weeks in jail before trial. During this time their children are frightened when they have to look at their parents through bulletproof glass barriers in austere visiting rooms. No physical contact is allowed. This is especially hard on toddlers and preschoolers (Prison Match 1983). If their single mother is the detainee, children may be shunted from one relative to another or from welfare shelter to foster home and back, since there is no way of knowing how long she will be in jail before her trial. Even when parents return home almost immediately, police procedures seldom take the children's stress into account. Attorneys are too busy, and pretrial investigations are structured to compile information about the culprit, not to assess the soundness of arrangements for the children's care.

Trial and Sentencing. Although children are seldom part of the trial and are usually not present when a parent is convicted and sentenced, reports in local news media may make their family troubles public knowledge. Some parents tell youngsters they are going away on vacation, going back to school, or taking a job in a distant location. These subterfuges add to children's stress and confusion, particularly when they are teased and bullied by classmates who know more than they do about their own parents.

Prison. Maintaining a relationship with an incarcerated parent is difficult for children. Frequently the correctional facility is located hundreds of miles from from home and visiting hours are restricted so that relatives cannot afford the time or money to bring youngsters to see their parents. When they do make the effort, even little children are treated as if they might be bringing in drugs or weapons. They have to talk with Dad or Mom through a screen or window and cannot hug or kiss. They can stay only a short time and most cry bitterly when they have to leave. Yet when children think back, it is reassuring to know their parents are well and still love them.

Infrequent visits and prison limits on incoming and outgoing phone calls make it difficult for caretakers to keep prisoners up to date on their children's progress and to consult about proposed changes in care. Youngsters feel abandoned and helpless when there is only brief, sporadic contact and when they are shunted from home to home without their parent's knowledge.

Recent research suggests that it is most stressful for children when a single mother is imprisoned. When a father is taken away, the household usually remains intact and the children stay in their mother's care. When there is no father to step in and help, single mothers, under stress during conviction and sentencing, make arrangements for their children which often prove to be less than satisfactory (Prison Match 1983). Often their children are moved from home to home, resulting in declining school achievement as they try to cope with new locations, people, and routines. There is the least stress when children are able to stay in their own homes with a relative or other trusted caretaker (Stanton 1980).

When a mother goes to prison and her children are placed in foster care, siblings may be separated from one another, removing them from an important source of love and support. To compound the insult, poor children's financial situations become even more precarious when their mother's wage-earning capacity ends.

Other stresses which children face during the period of incarceration include fights with their relatives, battles between their parents for legal custody, and the social stigma of being the child of a jailbird (Prison Match 1983). Some youngsters develop negative attitudes toward police and the law (Stanton 1980).

Release. Most correctional institutions do little to prepare inmates for their release. They do not keep track of prisoners' families, so parents may leave the facility without knowing where their children are living. Instead of a joyous homecoming, there is a tense and anxious time exacerbated by the adult's other worries. These include being unable to get a job, having no suitable place for the family to live, and having to wait weeks while the family's welfare status is established. Children, as always, respond to such parental stress with anxiety of their own. Experts rate the postrelease period as the most difficult time of all for youngsters.

Help for Children of Incarcerated Parents. In the late 1970s a number of groups were established throughout the United States with the express purpose of helping children cope with parental incarceration. The organizations persuaded a number of prison authorities to create appropriate visiting facilities and schedules. In some institutions, parents can spend whole days and weekends with their children, playing and assisting in academic and social development. In addition, attempts are now made to place children in foster homes near the prison. Support and counseling is provided for the family during the prison stay and after release. The experiences of these organizations and the recommendations of researchers (Stanton 1980) about ways to help children cope with parental incarceration are summarized in table 6–5.

Separation from Siblings

The average family living in the Unites States today has two children closely spaced in age and dependent on each other for companionship because their parents, both of whom work, spend limited time at home. Bank and Kahn (1982) believe that siblings tend to develop exceptionally strong bonds when they are together much of the day (as is usually the case when they are nearly the same age) and when their parents have relatively low levels of influence

Table 6–5
Ways to Help Children Cope with Parental Incarceration

Source of Stress	Ways to Help Children Cope
Arrest process	Work with local police to raise consciousness about children's needs when parent is arrested. Be sure police inquire about child care and allow parent to make necessary arrangements.
Pretrial period	Work with local courts and judges to broaden investigations to include suspect's family and its needs; improve visiting environments for children of detainees; encourage parent-child contact.
Imprisonment	Work with prisons to set up appropriate visiting hours and facilities for children. Request that youngsters be allowed to telephone parents in prison. Locate suitable foster placements close to institutions. Encourage a relative, neighbor, or teacher to be consistently available to the child to offer support and love. Provide counseling and social work assistance for inmates and their children.
Release	Offer counseling and social services to help inmate and family adjust. Work with local employers and landlords to increase availability of jobs and housing for parolees.

upon them. In these circumstances, children develop close, rather primitive relationships which they believe will last forever. They invent their own private languages and jokes and nominate one child to organize their activities. Although they may fight, they are basically loyal to one another. Closely knit twosomes and sibling groups make up for their brief contact with parents by functioning as definers of personality, teachers of new skills, and sources of comfort (Timberlake and Hamlin 1982). Thus, it is logical to predict that separation of cohesive sibling groups will be upsetting. Temporary loss of siblings through illness, physical or mental handicap, or foster placement, removes entertainers, protectors, and helpers, and leaves a vacuum.

Sibling Illness

When a sibling is hospitalized for an illness or operation, closely attached brothers and sisters empathize and feel as though they were going through the painful procedures themselves. They may be lonely and reflective and want to be by themselves for a while. This is expressed touchingly in a brief essay by a youngster from Appalachia who wrote about his loneliness when his brother went to the hospital. He spent the afternoon out in the yard listening to the birds and imagining that they came down and played with him dressed in their best clothes (Reed 1981).

When children are hospitalized, there are always major shifts in routines for their families. Parents have less time for the healthy siblings and demand more independence from them. Youngsters worry that they have caused the illness or will catch it themselves. They resent what appears to be the sick child's ability to get whatever he or she wants from their parents. Most of all, they miss the quality of companionship they had in the past. When they think of the ill sibling they feel a mixture of emotions: jealousy, anger, sadness, guilt, and fear. Children telegraph their distress through maladaptive coping strategies such as fighting with friends and siblings, wetting the bed at night, being afraid to leave the house, having headaches and stomachaches, being depressed, and doing poorly in school.

A number of organizations which deal regularly with the families of children who have chronic diseases, such as cancer, asthma, diabetes, and hemophilia, have developed techniques to assist healthy siblings. These methods have been used for many years with thousands of youngsters and are assumed to be effective, although they have not been tested scientifically. The following list summarizes the most frequently mentioned recommendations (Association for the Care of Children's Health 1982; National Cancer Institute 1980, 1982; Rosen 1979; Stearns 1979).

Make sure siblings have accurate information about the illness and know that they were in no way the cause. Update information frequently. Use repetition to insure understanding.

Be sure all of the children's close friends have accurate information.

Bring siblings to the hospital to visit the patient's room or clinic play area.

Help siblings to choose tasks they can do to care for the patient.

Prepare siblings for physical changes they will observe when the patient returns home; explain reasons and detail what the child will and will not be able to do.

Support siblings' feelings of sadness, crying; share your own grief with them.

Help siblings accept their negative feelings about being deprived of the patient's companionship and their parents' attention and care.

Continue normal daily routines and activities as much as possible. Respect siblings' need to participate in usual sports activities, visits with friends, parties, excursions.

Sibling's Physical or Mental Handicap

When a brother or sister is physically or mentally handicapped, there are potentially two kinds of separation which may be experienced by siblings. Sometimes the handicap is so severe that there are repeated hospitalizations or the child is institutionalized. These separations bring on all of the feelings of loss which occur when any family member is temporarily absent. In many cases however, the disabled youngster remains at home and the separation is psychological rather than physical. Healthy siblings yearn for a brother or sister who is like themselves, able to run and play, share fantasies, make mischief, and exclude adults (Featherstone 1980). They feel lonely and isolated from peers who misunderstand their "weird" sibling. Often it is the child who is closest in age to the disabled sibling who is most deeply affected (Chinitz 1981).

Retrospective accounts of home life with a handicapped sibling describe several positive outcomes for healthy brothers and sisters. These include experiences of being closer to their parents than most children; learning to cope with unfairness, sorrow, and anger relatively early in life; developing parenting skills; and knowing that they helped the disabled child to grow and be happy.

On the negative side, siblings have been observed to cope by taking out their anger on their parents or their toys, by regressing, acting out in school, or outwardly showing exaggerated love for the disabled sibling while inwardly feeling jealous and hateful. At the birth of a deformed infant, some young children feel guilt as they remember the times they bumped into their mother's belly while she was pregnant (Trout 1983). Pat Hartvigsen, staff member of an early intervention program for handicapped infants (pers. com. 1983) points out that elementary school age children are likely to worry about becoming disabled themselves and to fear that their brother or sister will die. They are embarrassed by the handicapped child's behavior; tearful when he or she destroys their favorite possessions and scribbles on their homework. Because their parents are protective, they are afraid to yell and express their anger. Older children may worry that responsibility for the disabled sibling will become theirs when their parents die. They may be reluctant to have children when they marry (Featherstone 1980).

Chinitz (1981) reports a group discussion with siblings of handicapped children which evoked a number of suggestions from youngsters. For example, when his parents were preoccupied with his disabled brother, one child deliberately stayed outdoors playing until the younger boy was in bed. Then his Mom and Dad had time to give him the attention he needed. Other children recommended keeping handicapped siblings from messing up books and papers by diverting their attention to substitute activities.

Chinitz and other practitioners find that children often know very little about the nature, treatment, and prognosis of their sibling's handicap. Few are helped to deal with teasing and other thoughtless reactions of neighbors and peers.

In some communities, respite services are available which allow families to take brief vacations with their healthy youngsters. Care is also provided while parents and siblings attend training sessions or meet with physicians and psychiatrists to improve their skills in working with the disabled child.

Foster Placement

One of the most traumatic of all temporary separations occurs for siblings when one child is taken out of the home and put into foster care or when the members of a sibling group are sent to different placements. There are no national or state figures on how often this happens, but researchers in a county near Washington, D.C., found that three-fourths of their local sibling groups had been separated for foster care placement (Timberlake and Hamlin 1982). Social agencies say they would like to keep sibling groups together. However, they point out that some foster homes have insufficient space to accommodate more than one child, and that foster parents need expensive extra support in order to deal effectively with two or more siblings. They also emphasize that special needs youngsters require trained foster parents and carefully designed facilities and that these homes usually have no space for normal brothers and sisters.

Children who remain at home when their siblings are placed in foster care often assume a heavy load of guilt. They see the foster placement as a punishment which they caused or at least should have prevented (Timberlake and Hamlin 1982).

On the other hand, when sibling groups are kept together, bonding theory suggests that the experience can be less stressful. Little research has been published on this subject, but one study by a New York City social agency found that siblings placed together were more likely to be permanently reunited with their parents than brothers and sisters who had been separated (Block 1981). Possible explanations for this finding take into account the potential power of the group to enable its members to survive under adverse conditions. Youngsters support one another in grieving for the absent parents. They create their own supply of warmth and reassurance. They maintain consistent relationships among themselves while they learn to adjust to the foster family. There are numerous examples in the clinical literature of siblings in wartime who apparently are able to give one another sufficient nurturing to make up for absent parents.

If children must be separated temporarily in foster care, common sense dictates that the youngsters be involved in the decision. During placement they need adult help in arranging for visits and telephone calls. Knowing the reason for their separation, maintaining contact while they are apart, and having some idea of how long the situation will last, all help to make foster care less stressful for siblings.

References

Allison, J., and J. Johnson, eds. 1981. *Say hi to Julie: A commentary from children in care in Alberta.* Calgary, Canada: Who Cares? A Society for Young People in Care.

Association for the Care of Children's Health. 1982. *The chronically ill child and family in the community.* Washington, D.C.

Aust, P.H. 1981. Using the life story book in treatment of children in placement. *Child Welfare*, 60:535–560.

Bank, S.P., and M.D. Kahn. 1982. *The sibling bond.* New York: Basic Books, Inc., Publishers.

Block, N.M. 1981. Toward reducing recidivism in foster care. *Child Welfare,* 60:597–609.

Bureau of the Census. 1982. *Marital status and living arrangements: March 1982.* Population Characteristics, Ser. P–20, no. 380. Washington, D.C.: Government Printing Office.

Cain, L.P., and N. Staver. 1976. Helping children adapt to parental illness. *Social Casework,* 57:575–580.

Children's Defense Fund. 1978. *Children without homes: An examination of public responsibility to children in out-of-home care.* Washington, D.C.

Chinitz, S.P. 1981. A sibling group for brothers and sisters of handicapped children. *Children Today,* November–December.

Clausen, J. 1979. The mentally ill at home: A family matter. In *Families today: A research sampler on families and children, Volume II,* ed. E. Corfman, NIMH. Washington, D.C.: Government Printing Office.

Featherstone, H. 1980. *A difference in the family: Living with a disabled child.* New York: Basic Books, Inc., Publishers.

Fein, E., A.N. Maluccio, V.J. Hamilton, and D.E. Ward. 1983. After foster care: Outcomes of permanency planning for children. *Child Welfare,* 62:485–558.

Fritsch, T.A., and J.D. Burkhead. 1981. Behavioral reactions of children to parental absence due to imprisonment. *Family Relations,* 30:83–88.

Getz, D. 1981. Focus on the abandoned child. United States Committee for UNICEF. *News of the World's Children,* December.

Gil, E., and K. Bogart. 1982. Foster children speak out: A study of children's perceptions of foster care. *Children Today,* January–February.

Goldstein, J., A. Freud, and A.J. Solnit. 1979. *Beyond the best interests of the child: New edition with epilogue.* New York: The Free Press, Macmillan Publishing Co., Inc.

Hillenbrand, E.D. 1976. Father absence in military families. *The Family Coordinator,* 25:451–458.

Hunter, E.J., and R.A. Hickman. 1981. *As parents go, so go the children: The adjustment and development of military children.* Report no. TR–USIU–81–01. San Diego: U.S. International University.

Irving, R. 1979. Helping uprooted children. Presentation at conference, Helping children to cope with stress, Lesley College, Cambridge, Mass., January.

Lexier, L.J. 1981. The problems of father absence: A preventative program. Paper presented in a symposium, *Down to the sea in ships: A study of father absence.* American Psychiatric Association meeting, May.

Mack, S. 1979. Helping children to cope with hospitalization. Presentation at conference, Helping children to cope with stress. Lesley College, Cambridge, Mass., January.

McGowan, B.G., and K.L. Blumenthal. 1978. *Why punish the children? A study of children of women prisoners.* Hackensack, N.J.: National Council on Crime and Delinquency.

National Cancer Institute. 1980. Department of Health and Human Services. *Coping with cancer: A resource for the health professional.* NIH 80–2080. Washington, D.C.: Government Printing Office.

————. 1982. Department of Health and Human Services. *Young people with cancer: A handbook for parents.* NIH 82–2378. Washington, D.C.: Government Printing Office.

Prison Match Staff. 1983. *Prison Match: A model program for imprisoned mothers and their children.* San Francisco: National Council on Crime and Deliquency. Mimeo.

Reed, J. 1981. Growing up in Appalachia. *Children Today*, January–February.

Rosen, S. 1979. Helping children to cope with chronic diseases. Presentation at conference, Helping children to cope with stress. Lesley College, Cambridge, Mass., January.

Rosenkrantz, L., and V. Joshua. 1982. Children of incarcerated parents: A hidden population *Children Today*, January–February.

Schor, E.L. 1982. The foster care system and health status of foster children. *Pediatrics*, 69:521–528.

Stanton, A.M. 1980. *When mothers go to jail.* Lexington, Mass.: Lexington Books, D.C. Heath and Company.

Stearns, N. 1979. Helping children to cope with cancer. Presentation at conference, Helping children to cope with stress. Lesley College, Cambridge, Mass., January.

Stein, J.M., and A.P. Derdeyn. 1980. The child in group foster care: Issues of separation and loss. *Journal of the American Academy of Child Psychiatry*, 19:90–100.

Sturges, J.S. 1978. Children's reactions to mental illness in the family *Social Casework*, 59:530–536.

Timberlake, E.M., and E.R. Hamlin, II. 1982. The sibling group: A neglected dimension of placement. *Child Welfare*, 61:545–552.

Trout, M.D. 1983. Birth of a sick or handicapped infant: Impact on the family. *Child Welfare*, 62:337–348.

White, R.W. 1974. Strategies of adaptation: An attempt at systematic description. In *Coping and Adaptation*, ed. G.V. Coelho, D.A. Hamburg, and J.E. Adams. New York: Basic Books, Inc., Publishers.

7 Divorce

Children experience divorce as a separation that is neither permanent nor temporary. The absent parent is lost but still living; he or she retains the title of mother or father, but never returns to the original parental role.

In the United States, 5,761,000 children under the age of eighteen live with divorced single parents. The number of children living with a divorced mother or father has more than doubled since 1970, and this at a time when the total number of children in the country declined by ten percent (Bureau of the Census 1982). Even this startlingly large number is incomplete, because the Census Bureau has not counted the hundreds of thousands of children who live with remarried mothers and fathers.

Effects of Divorce on Children

The many research reports which list children's negative reactions to divorce raise the question of whether youngsters would be better off if their battling parents stayed married. Hetherington (1979) maintains that "a conflict-ridden intact family is more deleterious to family members than is a stable home in which parents are divorced" (Hetherington 1979, 857). However, to date, no studies have measured and compared the stress levels of children whose parents divorce with the levels of those whose parents are hostile yet remain together "for the children's sake." We know that when parents separate in order to reduce marital discord, they generally continue to fight as they share the children in the years that follow. Some of their children report a lessening of tension. Others do not. The only children who are uniformly relieved by separation are those whose parents have been abusive to them (Wallerstein 1983).

Divorce is a process which takes several years and produces multiple stresses for youngsters. It begins when children first become aware that the marriage is in difficulty; when they find themselves witnessing more and more parental fights; or when they notice that communication between their parents has stopped. Next come intermittent separations and reunions. These lead eventually to a transition period when steps are taken to secure a legal separation and finally a divorce. After the decree, most children require from two to five years to recover their equilibrium (Ahrons 1983). Wallerstein and Kelly (1980) found that more than a third of the children they studied were thriving and another twenty-nine percent were in reasonably good shape by five years after the divorce. But a fairly large minority (thirty seven percent) were still moderately to severely depressed. It is important to recognize that the years of tension building up to the divorce, and the two to five years of adjustment which follow, can occupy a large fraction, even the totality, of a youngster's childhood.

When children's reactions to divorce are categorized by sex, research shows that boys are more negatively affected than girls (Hetherington 1979). Prior to the separation, parents are more likely to argue in front of boys than girls (Camara 1982). Even two years afterward, boys have more behavior problems at home and in school (Hetherington 1979). On the other hand, this effect may have been observed because most research has been limited to households headed by women. One of the few systematic comparisons of the effects of the sex of the custodial parent showed that father-custody boys and mother-custody girls were better adjusted than children who lived with opposite sex parents (Warshak and Santrock 1983).

Whether the resident parent is a mother or a father, divorce brings important microsystem changes, especially in adult-child relationships. Live-in parents often become more authoritarian, while noncustodial fathers and mothers become more relaxed (albeit less available). It is typical for both adults to lower their standards for their children's behavior and school achievement. Parents may experience difficulty in communicating with their youngsters, in showing affection, and in maintaining consistent discipline. In return, angry children may try to manipulate the grownups, using the animosities they know exist between them (Kurdek 1981). Sibling groups may draw closer together for reassurance and comfort as older children watch out for younger ones and become sensitive to the feelings of any sibling left home alone (Allers 1982).

Exosystem pressures for divorced children include separation from their friends and changing homes and schools. Midweek and weekend visits with the noncustodial parent leave little time for homework (Allers 1982). Custodial mothers frequently have less money to spend as the family's socioeconomic status is reduced from middle to lower class (Kurdek 1981).

In contrast, the macrosystem offers support to the divorcing family. Society today sees divorce as preferable to an unhappy marriage because of the prevalent belief that parental fighting is damaging to children. Separation is expected to produce an environment which will be more peaceful and healthy for youngsters (Kurdek 1981). National television shows promote the stereotype of children living happily with their single and remarried divorced parents.

Children's Conceptions of Divorce

Central to the way in which children respond to divorce is their understanding of this abstract idea. A recent study by Neal (1983) provides a tentative yet convincing basis for a series of age-stage descriptions of children's understanding of the concept. He interviewed and tested a small sample of forty-four children whose parents were separated and intending to divorce, and found that these youngsters constructed illogical yet sensible beliefs about what was happening to their families.

Three- to Six-Year-Olds. As might be expected, Neal describes three- to six-year-old children as egocentric and personal in their thinking. They measure love by the physical distance between people. A parent who moves away from them does not like them. They cannot understand the usual explanation given by parents that "Daddy didn't leave you, he left Mommy." Further, these little ones rate their own behavior as good if it is acceptable to a parent and bad if it elicits punishment. Using their illogical yet sensible reasoning, they believe that something they did was bad and caused their parent to go away; that is, dislike of the child caused the parent to go away and in turn the dislike was caused by the youngster's bad behavior.

Five- to Eight-Year-Olds. Neal finds early elementary school youngsters still egocentric and personal, but now also aware of the conflicts between their parents. Illogically yet sensibly, they believe that their own behavior caused fights between their parents and these fights resulted in the decision to divorce. They also believe the situation is reversible. If something they did caused the rupture, then there is something they can do to make their parents reconcile. They also think that when the noncustodial parent doesn't come to see them it is because he or she didn't enjoy the previous visit. They believe that if children make their absent parents happy, they will be rewarded with more frequent and longer contact. If they fail, the missing parent will probably find some other child to love.

Nine- to Twelve-Year-Olds. Neal finds that nine- to twelve-year-olds can understand that their parents have inner as well as surface feelings. They recognize that the adults can change and no longer be in love. Most children do not understand why this happens and make the assumption that something has gone wrong at home which can be remedied if their parents will only try hard enough. Their illogical yet sensible belief is that a recent family event has caused the break, so changes can be made to restore love. Children of this age are in the process of learning their own hard lessons about having to compromise and share. They assume that parents are simply being selfish if they don't reconcile their differences.

If we accept Neal's version of young children's thinking about divorce, we have a framework for understanding why they have so much difficulty in comprehending "civilized" separations where parents remain friendly yet still divorce (Futterman 1980). Neal's framework can also explain the Wallerstein and Kelly (1980) finding that miserably unhappy parents who want to split up often discover, to their astonishment, that their children are satisfied with family life "as is." Obviously, during the divorce process, the perceptions of children and their parents are discrepant, even when the adults communicate freely with the youngsters and attempt to involve them in family decisions. Children's levels of cognition preclude the kind of reasoning needed to deal with concepts which seem crystal clear to grownups.

The remainder of this chapter summarizes the major conclusions on which there is general agreement regarding children's reactions to the stresses which occur at each stage of divorce. Suggestions for ways of helping children cope have been gleaned from research, from reports written by children who have experienced divorce, and from practitioners who work with troubled families. While they seem on surface inspection to be effective, to date, none of these coping strategies have been tested scientifically.

Stage One: Troubled Marriage

When their marriage is in deep trouble, parents are likely to withdraw from each other into icy silence or to go to the other extreme of fighting and violence.

Preschool children seldom recognize the first stage of the divorce process. They focus on their own interactions with Mom and Dad and are generally unaware of the interactions between the adults.

School-age children notice that their parents are antagonistic. Their responses vary according to the way in which the adults conduct their marital battles. When parents stop communicating with each other and contain their hostility behind closed doors, children are insulated from the problem and get used to the cold, muted anger. Most come to believe that all mothers and fathers behave the way theirs do. As the tension increases, however, children sense and sometimes participate in the war they feel between their elders, becoming irritable, loud, and aggressive. Others create crises to break the silence and force their parents to talk to each other (Rosenzweig 1979).

When parental fighting is out in the open, children are frightened that one or the other will get hurt. Some feel they must choose between mother and father and defend that person against the spouse. Youngsters who are sure they caused the conflict try to be peacemakers. A few withdraw into corners and resolve to be very good so they won't give their parents any cause for further arguments. Unconsciously they may find ways to become ill or get into trouble to divert their parents' attention from their bickering (Rosenzweig 1979).

The Kids' Book of Divorce (Rofes 1982) suggests a number of ways in which children can cope with their parents' fighting. They are urged to leave the room when anger explodes and to be careful not to interrupt lest they become the objects of the battle. Children who have successfully coped with this stage advise others to talk with a trusted adult friend or relative about their feelings. If that is not possible, one youngster suggests venting anger and fear by writing a book, a diary, or a poem.

Stage Two: Separation(s)

At this point in the marriage, the partners feel the need to put some physical space between themselves in order to find out if they will be more content living apart than together. One parent moves out on a trial basis. Sometimes he or she never comes back, but in most cases, there follow a series of partings and reunions over a period of several years.

Preschoolers are bewildered by the separations. Each leave-taking seems to be final. Each departure, in the minds of the children, proves that the parent no longer loves them. Many youngsters regress and develop anxiety around leaving Mom or Dad even long enough to go to sleep.

School-age children panic and fear that the parent who has just slammed out of the house will never return. When they visit him or her they find it hard to make the transition from the accustomed environment and relationship to the furnished room and unsettled lifestyle. Their contacts may turn into a series of trips to zoos and amusement parks accompanied by unexpected presents as though every day was Christmas (Rofes 1982). Children feel rejection, anger, and disdain for both parents who seem to them to be selfish because they won't settle their differences (Futterman 1980). At home they have to restructure their routines and take on new roles in order to cope with the loss of one parent. When the parent returns, everything has to be rearranged again. The result is that children have a sense of being always out of balance (Ahrons 1980). A few attempt to cope by keeping their antennae urgently tuned to their parents. They have a constant need to know what they can do to be more acceptable to the grownups (Futterman 1980).

Even therapists have few suggestions for ways of helping children handle the stress of this second stage of divorce. Rosenzweig (1979) encourages families to sit down together in advance of each separation and plan together so that the children know (1) where each parent will live, (2) how the youngsters will be taken care of, (3) how often they will be able to visit the parent who is leaving, and (4) how long the separation will last. Children who have lived through stage two warn their peers to be prepared; life will probably be very hard before their parents finally decide to separate for good (Rofes 1982).

Stage Three: Transition and Legal Steps

In stage three, both parents are overwhelmed by the details of working with lawyers, finding new places for each to live, dividing their property, agreeing on custody, and making a financial settlement. They are intensely busy and preoccupied with their own concerns. They have little energy for parenting and may physically and emotionally neglect their children during this period (Rosenzweig 1979). Hetherington and her associates (1978) describe these households as *disordered*, and custodial mothers as short-tempered and attempting to control their children through coercion.

Preschool children cope with stress by regressing to more infantile patterns. They lose bladder and bowel control; refuse solid food; become tearful, irritable, and unusually dependent. They fear adandonment. Sleep disturbances are common. They become more aggressive and seem unable to get any pleasure from their play (Wallerstein 1983).

Six- to eight-year-olds are preoccupied with and grieve openly for the lost parent. They long intensely for his or her return and fear that the absent parent will find some other child to love. Their sadness leads to moderate depresssion for some. The stress they experience at home spills over and disrupts their ability to learn in school and to maintain their old friendships. Many youngsters are aware that they are burdensome to their busy parents. They attempt to cope by denying that anything is wrong at home, by developing physical complaints, having trouble sleeping, being moody and sulky. Some experts identify this as the most difficult stage of the divorce process for six- to eight-year-olds (Rosenzweig 1979; Wallerstein 1983).

Nine- to twelve-year-olds are angry at both of their parents and frequently express their feelings directly. When they see a mother or father hurt and crying, they feel overwhelmingly lonely and confused. They recognize that everyone in the family is upset and hard to live with (Rofes 1982). At this age they are aware of, stimulated by, and distracted by their parents' sexuality and dating behavior (Wallerstein 1983). As with younger children, their schoolwork suffers and some develop minor ailments. Many are embarrassed to tell their friends about the impending divorce and yet are anxious to know how other children have dealt with the problems they are now facing.

There is general agreement about two basic ways to help children cope with the stress of this stage of divorce (Ahrons 1980; Allers 1982; Hetherington 1979; Rofes 1982; Wallerstein 1983). First, it is essential for both parents to talk directly with the children and let them know exactly what is going to happen to the family. Divorced children urge parents to break the news to all of the siblings at the same time. Following this, they suggest that older brothers and sisters be given time alone with their parents to ask questions and clarify issues. In their experience, well-informed older children can help younger ones, because they are better at explaining things than grownups (Rofes 1982). Wallerstein (1983) warns, however, that preschoolers and younger elementary-age children not be given information about the divorce too far in advance. Because their time sense is undeveloped, when nothing happens right away, they may believe that the divorce news was only an ugly fantasy. When the event finally takes place, they may feel that their most awful nightmare has become real.

The second essential is that children know that they will have plenty of opportunities to be with the noncustodial parent and that visits will follow a regular schedule. When this is not going to be the case, they need a thorough explanation of the reasons why they will see less of that parent.

Other suggestions for helping children cope with the transitional stage of divorce include involving them in discussions with age-mates who have gone through the process (Kurdek 1981) and helping them to find sports or hobbies to absorb their attention and deflect it from the problems at home.

Some children advise eleven- and twelve-year-olds to learn as much as they can about the details of the legal separation agreement. They feel it is reassuring to know what arrangements have been made for the children's support, education, and living quarters, and what will happen when they reach adult status at age eighteen (Rofes 1982).

Allers (1982) has written a book specifically for teachers in which he contends that the sameness of daily events and relationships in school is comforting to children whose families are in chaos. Adults can expect these youngsters to panic and misbehave when there are changes in routines or when there is a substitute teacher. Yet, standards of achievement and behavior need to be maintained. He urges teachers to make themselves available to listen to children's problems and concerns and to use books and stories to initiate class discussions about divorce. When gifts are made to be sent home, both father and mother should be included. Conferences should be scheduled with and reports sent to both parents.

Stage Four: Divorce and Aftermath

The largest body of research has concentrated on the stresses which children experience during stage four when the divorce becomes final and the family adjusts to a new pattern of living. Parents establish separate domiciles and custodial mothers leave home each day to look for or work at jobs. Usually both adults have less time to spend with the children, are less patient, and less able than in the past to maintain predictable household routines. Children are likely to live in new neighborhoods and attend different schools. They must learn how to travel between the two households and get used to the different demands of each. They also become witnesses to the adults' sexual and dating behavior.

Immediate Reactions to Divorce

In their first reports of what has now become a ten-year longitudinal study of children of divorce, Wallerstein and Kelly (1975) identify reactions which are typical for children at the time of the final decree. Toddlers ranging in age from thirty to thirty-nine months regress in toilet training, become fearful, and shed a lot of tears. They have trouble sleeping and are irritable. They are confused about what is happening to their parents and inclined to temper tantrums. In addition to exhibiting most of the same reactions, preschoolers understand the divorce to have been caused by their own behavior. In nursery school they become aggressive and simultaneously afraid of youngsters who attack them in return. Five- and six-year-olds seem to proceed at their usual pace of development, neither regressing nor losing ground in school. Other researchers have not corroborated the Wallerstein and Kelly findings for five- and six-year-olds, but instead record interruptions in developmental tasks (Chethik and Kalter 1980).

Older children report that some of the stresses they remember from the first days after the divorce include having to take younger siblings to visit the noncustodial parent, having to think about their parents' money problems, being alone a lot, and particularly having to do housework by themselves. They remember being afraid to tell their friends about the divorce because it might turn them into outcasts (Rofes 1982). Children who have to move to new locations and make new friends often turn inward, at least at first, and guard their feelings against further pain. Some of the most severely stressed youngsters appear to be the ones who are employed as messengers and spies between their still-warring parents (Futterman 1980).

Society is beginning to develop rituals around divorce which may help children accept and cope with the inevitable. For example, Rabbi Earl Grollman (1981) offers families a divorce ceremony. In front of the assembled children and relatives, the uncoupled adults promise to try to forgive each other and to do their utmost to be successful parents even though they have failed as marriage partners.

Scheiner, Musetto, and Cordier (1982) suggest that in the first weeks after divorce, children need to be told over and over again that it is okay to love both parents. They suggest too that grandparents, aunts, and uncles maintain their relationships with the youngsters. The authors have designed custody and visitation counseling sessions during which adults and children cooperatively work out differences and come to mutual agreements.

Older divorced children have several suggestions for helping their peers cope with the first days after the divorce. They suggest that teachers, counselors, and parents remember that they are only kids; that even when they know all the rules in each household, they will surely make some mistakes during the first weeks in each. They feel that it should even be legitimate to stay home for a day or two to get used to their new surroundings (Rofes 1982).

The First Year

One year after the divorce, Wallerstein and Kelly (1975) find toddlers generally returning to their normal behaviors except that some are too quick to seek physical contact with strange adults. Preschoolers also adjust by the end of the first twelve months. Those children who do not, tend to stall at the developmental stage they were in at the time of the divorce. Research in the 1980s seems to negate some of the optimistic first-year adjustment reports of Wallerstein and Kelly's preschoolers. Kurdek (1981) summarizes recent studies which indicate that young children still have nightmares, sleep disturbances, depressed appetite, inhibition of playfulness, and feelings of guilt after twelve months have passed. Many are lonely. Nursery and kindergarten teachers note that a year after the divorce, their pupils still have unusually short attention spans (Camara 1982).

All researchers agree that during this first postdivorce year, elementary school youngsters suffer disruptions in their ability to learn. Problems with concentration lead them to need repeated explanations (Kurdek 1981). Parents who are overburdened with work and child care responsibilities may fail to provide the kind of support and challenge that spurs children to keep up with their school work. One study finds that when a family does not have a regular schedule for the noncustodial parent's visits, the more frequent his or her surprise appearances become, the more poorly the child does in school (Isaacs 1983). At home, both custodial parents and children suffer from too much of one another's company. They are easily annoyed with behavior that used to go unnoticed (Rosenzweig 1979). Divorced children report being highly uncomfortable trying to talk on the phone with Mom or Dad while the other parent is in the room (Rofes 1982). In addition, parental expectations that one of the children should take over the missing spouse's role create further stress (see chapter 3).

Quite a number of interventions have been designed to help children cope with the first year after a divorce. While there are no objective measures of the effectiveness of these strategies, most children say that they feel better for having taken part, especially because they have learned that they are not alone in their distress (Camara 1982).

Possibly because there is a realization that parents cannot offer their children sufficient help in coping with the stresses of this first postdivorce year, many communities expect teachers to take over a portion of the task. Classroom group discussions of this subject are common. Even nursery school teachers read stories about divorced youngsters to their groups. Camara (1982) warns, however, that books must be chosen carefully to be sure that the author affirms the pain that children experience. Too often youngsters are portrayed as living a carefree life with a single divorced parent. Children who are hurt and unhappy with their parents' divorce may wonder why they are so different from the children in the stories.

Teachers who work with preschoolers whose parents have been divorced may find that a series of absences or late arrivals signal the child's need for additional support in dealing with a chaotic home. When under stress, kindergartners may become hesitant to join in group play without first spending a lot of time looking on. Then they precipitate themselves into the activity by aggressively trying to take a role already held by another child. Their peers assume that anyone who hestitates to join them and then acts bossy really doesn't like them and doesn't want to play (Camara 1982). Teachers can help when they observe these interpersonal difficulties. Role-playing and discussions with the class about ways of joining ongoing games may alleviate the problem.

Teachers in the elementary grades note that older children show their distress by coming to school late, being preoccupied in class, not doing their homework, being aggressive, hanging around school in the afternoon, and expresssing anger in their writing or art work. Most regain their balance when they are held to the same standards as the other children rather than coddled. They appreciate a teacher who listens to their concerns yet does not make judgments about their families. Rosenzweig (1979) suggests that teachers help youngsters to express their feelings through creative projects. They can also teach sublimation as a coping style by getting children involved in hobbies and sports.

At present, society's most fashionable solution to children's problems with the first year of divorce is to pressure parents to undertake joint custody; that is, they should arrange for each former partner to spend equal time with the children and to take equal responsibility for their upbringing. When this is successful, youngsters report themselves almost as satisfied as if their parents had stayed together. Teachers and couselors claim that joint custody produces better adjustment in school and with peers. However, joint custody is a difficult process when antagonism exists between the divorced couple.

Clinicians suggest that many children who live with single parents can benefit from brief counseling or play sessions with a trained therapist of the same sex as the missing parent. Once helped to accept their yearning and to express their anger, youngsters quickly recoup developmental losses (Chethik and Kalter 1980).

Three to Five Years Postdivorce

Several years after the divorce, children who never see their noncustodial parents are the least well-adjusted in school and at home. Those who have regular contact are likely to complain about the bother of having to live in two households (Ahrons 1983). Five years after the divorce, a third of Wallerstein and Huntington's (1983) sample of divorced mothers and children are struggling to make ends meet. Seven percent have recently become welfare recipients. Financial worries are common. When Dad's checks don't arrive as expected, children blame their mothers. And some fathers in this study add to their children's stress by insisting that youngsters earn their child-support money by doing major household chores during their visits.

When parents remarry, some children experience stress and others are comforted. One study found that remarried noncustodial fathers tend to favor the new spouse's progeny and to decrease the amount of support for and number of visits to their biological youngsters (Wallerstein and Huntington 1983). The children who receive diminished attention and financial support feel their loss keenly. Alternatively, for the stepchildren, the presence of a second parent in the house can help to reduce stress and provide sustenance. In some cases, gaining a stepparent correlates with increased school achievement (Furstenberg 1983). Wallerstein and Kelly (1980) note that boys who form loving relationships with their stepfathers make rapid developmental gains.

The least fortunate youngsters appear to be those who live through a divorce, a remarriage, and then another divorce. They consistently have more trouble in school than children whose parents have been divorced only once (Furstenberg 1983).

By the end of five years, most children have accepted the reality of their changed family status, are making steady progress in school, and are building networks of friends. Their parents are settled and reasonably calm, so household schedules are predictable and the children receive good physical and emotional care (Wallerstein 1983).

Three to five years after the divorce, teachers and counselors have little therapeutic contact with the majority of youngsters. Only the most severely damaged are still in therapy. However, when schools and community agencies organize peer counseling groups, they find considerable interest and participation among "old timers," as well as children new to divorce. Girls in particular are eager to join. Boys seem less prone to discuss their feelings. In later adolescence, when both sexes begin to question their own desires for marriage and children, divorce discussions again seem useful, no matter how long ago the family separation occurred.

References

Ahrons, C.R. 1980. Divorce: A crisis of family transition and change. *Family Relations,* 29:533–540.

————. 1983. The binuclear family: A three-year followup analysis. Paper presented at conference, Divorce fallout: What happens to the kids? Sixtieth annual meeting of the American Orthopsychiatric Association, Boston.

Allers, R.D. 1982. *Divorce, children, and the school.* Princeton, N.J.: Princeton Book Company, Publishers.

Bureau of the Census. 1982. *Marital status and living arrangements; March 1982.* Population Characteristics, Ser. P-20, no. 380. Washington, D.C.: Government Printing Office.

Camara, K.A. 1982. The experience of parental divorce for young children: Implications for the school and the community. Paper presented at 1982 New England Kindergarten Conference, Randolph, Mass.

Chethik, M., and N. Kalter. 1980. Developmental arrest following divorce: The role of therapist as a developmental facilitator. *Journal of the American Academy of Child Psychiatry,* 19:281–288.

Furstenberg, F. 1983. Divorce and child adjustment. Paper presented at conference, Current research in divorce and remarriage. Sixtieth annual meeting of the American Orthopsychiatric Association, Boston.

Futterman, E.H. 1980. Child psychiatry perspectives: After the "civilized" divorce. *Journal of the American Academy of Child Psychiatry,* 19:525–530.

Grollman, E. 1981. A conversation with Fred Rogers and Earl Grollman. In *Talking with families about divorce.* Pittsburgh: Family Communications, Inc.

Hetherington, E.M. 1979. Divorce: A child's perspective. *American Psychologist,* 34:851–858.

Hetherington, E.M., M. Cox, and R. Cox. 1978. The aftermath of divorce. In *Mother-child relations,* ed. J.H. Stevens, Jr. and M. Mathews. Washington, D.C.: National Association for the Education of Young Children.

Isaacs, M. 1983. Outcome for children of divorce: A family perspective. Paper presented at conference, Divorce fallout: What happens to the kids? Sixtieth annual meeting of the American Orthopsychiatric Association, Boston.

Kurdek, L.A. 1981. An integrative perspective on children's divorce adjustment. *American Psychologist,* 36:856–866.

Neal, J.J. 1983. Children's understanding of their parents' divorces. In *Children and divorce,* ed. L.A. Kurdek. New Directions for Child Development, no. 19. San Francisco: Jossey-Bass Inc., Publishers.

Rofes, E.E. ed. 1982. *The kids' book of divorce: By, for and about kids.* New York: Vintage Books, division of Random House.

Rosenzweig, H. 1979. Helping chldren to cope with their parents' divorce. Presentation at conference, Helping Children to cope with stress, Lesley College, Cambridge, Mass., January.

Scheiner, L.C., A.P. Musetto, and D.C. Cordier. 1982. Custody and visitation counseling: A report of an innovative program. *Family Relations,* 31:99–107.

Wallerstein, J.S. 1983. Children of divorce: Stress and developmental tasks. In *Stress, coping and development in children,* ed. N. Garmezy and M. Rutter. New York: McGraw-Hill Book Company.

Wallerstein, J.S., and D. Huntington. 1983. Non-financial factors in fathers' post-divorce economic support of their children. Paper presented at conference, Divorce fallout: What happens to the kids? Sixtieth annual meeting of the American Orthopsychiatric Association, Boston.

Wallerstein, J.S., and J.B. Kelly. 1975. The effects of parental divorce: Experiences of the preschool child. *Journal of the American Academy of Child Psychiatry,* 14:600–616.

————. 1980. *Surviving the break-up: How parents and children cope with divorce.* New York: Basic Books, Inc. Publishers.

Warshak, R.A., and J.W. Santrock. 1983. The impact of divorce in father-custody and mother-custody homes: The child's perspective. In *Children and divorce,* ed. L.A. Kurdek. New Directions for Child Development, no. 19. San Francisco: Jossey-Bass Inc., Publishers.

8

Physical and Emotional Abuse

Definition of Abuse

The severe stress of child abuse has been a national media issue since the mid-1970s and continues today as a major subject for research. An incidence and severity study funded by the National Center on Child Abuse and Neglect (1981), counted the number of cases from May 1979 to June 1980 which met the following criteria:

> A child maltreatment situation is one where, through purposive acts or marked inattention to the child's basic needs, behavior of a parent/substitute or other adult caretaker caused foreseeable and avoidable injury or impairment to a child or materially contributed to unreasonable prolongation or worsening of an existing injury or impairment (National Center on Child Abuse and Neglect 1981, 4).

The study, which omitted instances of abuse by siblings and by institutional personnel, found 652,000 maltreated youngsters under the age of eighteen in the United States. Of these, 207,000 had been physically assaulted and 138,400 emotionally abused. Approximately equal numbers of boys and girls, blacks and whites, were found in their reports. Rural and urban children were at slightly greater risk than suburban youngsters. Six of every one-thousand children under the age of five were abused. Children ages six to twelve were maltreated at the higher rate of eleven per thousand.

The study further estimated that one-thousand children were killed by parents or caretakers in 1979–80, which is an average of nearly three youngsters a day. Of these, seventy-two percent died of injuries and twenty-eight percent of physical neglect. The majority of children who died (seventy-four percent) were five years old or younger. Six- to twelve-year-olds were more likely to be severely injured than killed, perhaps because the same action which kills a toddler only incapacitates an older child.

In nearly half of the cases reported to the National Center on Child Abuse and Neglect, the abuse was perpetrated by both parents in concert. Biological mothers and fathers were most frequently the aggressors. Other abusive caretakers included stepfathers, paramours, and adult relatives residing in the household.

These statistics paint a conservative picture of the extent of the problem. Other estimates are a good deal higher (Starr 1979), generally based on the premise that many cases exist that remain unreported.

Sibling Abuse.

The same injuries that would warrant a charge of child abuse against a parent are generally ignored when they are committed by a sibling. In their study of family violence, Straus, Gelles, and Steinmetz (1980) found that severe sibling abuse had occurred in more than half of their sample families during the research year. The authors suggest that such abuse is not reported because society views battles between siblings as a normal part of growing up. As a result, untold numbers of youngsters live in fear, "weaponless and without safe refuge," in their own homes (Tooley 1977, 26). Tooley describes three patterns common to parents who do not protect their younsters from sibling abuse. These are: (1) ignoring or denying that the abuse exists, (2) placating a violent child by failing to protect siblings from his or her attacks, or (3) subtly encouraging increased sibling conflict so that children will act out the parents' violent impulses.

Institutional Abuse

Many training schools, detention centers, and children's shelters use disciplinary techniques that clearly fit definitions of abuse. Staff members beat and humiliate youngsters. In 1979 in New Jersey, at a time when that state was attempting to eliminate child abuse from its institutions, 339 cases of staff assaults on youngsters were reported (Corrigan 1981).

Almost every school, center, or shelter has what is euphemistically called a time out or meditation room where children are placed in locked, solitary confinement, sometimes naked and without toilet facilities. The experience is supposed to calm them and improve their behavior (Miller 1981). College student volunteers who locked themselves in their own comfortable bedrooms for only twenty-four hours experienced extreme emotional discomfort. They rated isolation as a serious form of abuse. Yet, in institutions, children may be kept in isolation rooms for several days at a time.

Most definitions of abuse are designed to facilitate case finding and thus are broad enough to include all known forms of maltreatment. For the purposes of this book, however, definitions focus on the child's point of view. To young victims, abuse and neglect involve completely different relationships with adult caretakers. Abuse implies an active emotional connection between aggressor and child. Neglect, on the other hand, is experienced as adult withdrawal and as nonrecognition of the child's needs. In this chapter then, abuse is defined as *any physically or emotionally damaging attempt to shape or change a child's behavior or personality.* The aggressor maintains contact with the child and the youngster remains attached to the abuser.

The Ecology of Abuse

Whether the abuse is physical or emotional, maltreated children live in similar environments. The microsystem denies them a sense of security and self-esteem. The exosystem fails to supply friendship and support. The macrosystem encourages adults to use corporal punishment against them and reminds them that they are their parents' private property.

Microsystem Dynamics.

Current theories contend that children whose personalities or physical needs mismatch with those of their parents contribute to their own maltreatment (Belsky 1980, Starr 1979). Parental irritation with a child's normal behavior triggers the impulse to abuse. While most adults are able to control such internal urges to violence, abusive parents are likely to attack the child if they (1) have low frustration tolerance, (2) hold unrealistic expectations for children, (3) are under stress, and (4) have experienced abuse in their own childhoods. When youngsters respond to punishment with defiance, a cycle of punitive interactions is initiated. For example, three-year-old Heather's mother always slept after lunch and insisted that Heather do so too. But Heather needed little rest and was unable to sleep one afternoon. Awakened by noisy play, Heather's mother felt she had been deliberately disturbed and retaliated by locking the youngster in the bathroom. Heather turned the area into a shambles. Her mother then burned Heather's hands by holding them against a hot radiator until she promised to clean up the room and go back to bed.

Infants who are most likely to be abused include those who are born prematurely, have any kind of handicap, are irritable, have irregular sleep-wake cycles, are colicky, or are unwanted by their parents (Belsky 1980; Starr 1979; Watkins and Bradbard 1982). As they get older, children who are handicapped, hyperactive, or intellectually much slower or much brighter than other members of the family are also at risk of abuse.

Exosystem Factors

Abusive families often are isolated (or isolate themselves) from relatives and potential friends. Thus, maltreated youngsters have little experience in socializing and often don't know how to make friends in school. In addition, their parents may discourage peer attachments (Garbarino and Gilliam 1980). This combination of factors eliminates the extrafamilial sources of warmth and support which most children enjoy. The neighborhoods in which abusive families find housing offer little support to children. Often clusters of maltreated youngsters live near one another (Garbarino and Gilliam 1980). Even middle- and upper-class abused children lack significant exosystem supports. For example, several authors maintain that private family physicians defer to parents rather than advocating for their child patients. They are apt to diagnose an injured child as accident-prone instead of abused (Newberger and Hyde 1979). This is especially true in cases where the doctor is familiar with the parents (McPherson and Garcia 1983).

Macrosystem Pressures

On television, in school, and on the streets, maltreated children are aware that physical aggression is a socially accepted way of solving problems and dealing with misbehavior. After all, the United States Supreme Court has ruled that schools can use corporal punishment on children (Belsky 1980). Society reinforces abused youngsters' beliefs that adults or siblings who hurt them are right to do so. They know themselves to be bad, thus the assaults against them are justified (Fraiberg, Adelson, and Shapiro 1975). Society also confirms the abuser's belief that children are their parents' private property, to be disciplined and brought up as the adults see fit, without interference by outsiders.

Identifying Abuse Victims

It is difficult to accurately identify maltreated youngsters. Few are willing to advertise their misery to outsiders and most deny mistreatment when questioned. Signs of physical abuse are obviously easier to see than the subtle ravages of verbal and emotional assault, but there are ways in which a careful observer can gather information leading to a reasonable hypothesis of either form of abuse.

Physical Abuse

Children's experiences of physical abuse encompass the full range of human savagery. They are beaten, burned, and thrown against walls, down stairs, and out of windows. They are tortured, locked in closets, tied to beds and chairs, and assaulted with guns, clubs, and knives. They are deprived of food, sleep, shelter, and schooling. They are required to deny their own urgent needs in favor of gratifying those of the aggressor. They are imprisoned in webs of unreasonable and inconsistent rules and brutally punished when these are broken.

Physically abusive parents usually ignore good behavior and are unable to express pleasure in their children (Galdston 1979). Discipline techniques are both inconsistent and unreasonably harsh. Most of these parents love their children yet hate, reject, and resent them at the same time.

Halperin (1981) claims that in addition to abuse victims, brothers and sisters are also traumatized by the assaults they observe. Siblings who witness physical abuse, even though they are not themselves objects of parental violence, apparently are emotionally damaged by the experience. She finds that victims and siblings express the same ambivalent or negative feelings about their parents.

Symptoms of Physical Abuse

Obvious symptoms of physical abuse include bruises and welts which may reflect the shape of the object used to beat the youngster; burns (especially those made by boiling water or cigarettes) on soles, palms, back, or buttocks; broken bones; and cuts and bruises. Elementary school children who insist on wearing sweaters, hats, or coats in warm schoolrooms may do so to hide their injuries. In general, abused youngsters are often inappropriately dressed for the weather or the situation. Some children may have a sudden hearing loss. Others may be undernourished or dehydrated, or report being forced to drink alcohol or take drugs. In infants, there may be evidence of starvation or failure to thrive.

When there are no visible signs of abuse, practitioners turn to observations of behavior patterns which have been found to be typical of abused children. A combination of two or three of the following indicators can serve as a danger signal that physical abuse may be present. Table 8–1 summarizes the findings of a number of authors (Broadhurst 1979; Elmer and Gregg 1979; Galdston 1979; Gardner 1975; Gill 1982; Green 1978; Helfer and Kempe 1972; Martin 1972; Parents Anonymous 1983; Watkins and Bradbard 1982).

Emotional Abuse

Emotional abuse is always a part of the process of physical abuse. However, it is also a subtle form of maltreatment in its own right when practiced by parents who would never dream of hitting or injuring their youngsters (Herbruck 1979).

Emotional maltreatment occurs when adults *attempt to shape children's behavior through the use of severe disparagement, humiliation, rejection,*

Table 8-1
Behavior Patterns of Physically Abused Children

Behavior Category	Age 5 and Under	Age 6 to 12
Expressiveness and apparent sense of self	Bland affect, no tears, no laughter No curiosity/exploration Unable to play; no sense of joy Shows no affect when attacking another child Afraid of dark, being hurt, being alone Reluctant to try messy activities Aggressive, hyperactive, or withdrawn	Has few opinions, no strong likes or dislikes Impulsive or inhibited and unable to be spontaneous Low self-esteem Either aggressive or withdrawn Seems stuck in an early stage of emotional development
Response to frustration or adversity	Withdraws or has tantrum	Low tolerance; requires immediate gratification
Language and learning	Lack of speech or delayed language development Delayed motor development Short attention span	Learning disabilities Speech impediments Poor memory Declining academic ability
Relationships with peers	Grabs objects from others without trying to retain them Inept social skills Avoids or is aggressive toward peers Can't wait or take turns	Feels different from peers and doesn't know how to make friends Apprehensive when others cry Tries to control, exploit, manipulate peers to get things, services Blames others when things go wrong
Relationships with parents	Shows no expectation of being comforted; no distress at separation Alert for danger Solicitous of parent's needs Constantly aware of parent's reactions May defy parent's commands Difficult to toilet train	Suspicious, mistrustful behavior mirrors that of parents Talks glowingly (if unrealistically) about home and parents Solicitous of parent's needs Does not turn to parent for comfort

Table 8-1 (continued)

Behavior Category	Age 5 and Under	Age 6 to 12
Relationships with other adults	Relates indiscriminately to adults in charming and agreeable ways; seeks affection from any adult Avoids being touched Responds negatively to praise Always seems to want/need more objects, attention, etc	Solicitous and agreeable or suspicious and mistrustful Tries to control and manipulate to obtain food and favors Does not respond to praise and positive attention Does not respond to limits Avoids being touched

guilt, and fear. Abused children are constantly told that they are no good. They are criticized and held to impossible standards. Parental discipline is inconsistent, involving bizarre punishments (being made to eat out of the dog's dish on the floor as retribution for poor table manners) or public humiliation (wearing a sign pinned to a jacket advertisng "I am a liar"). Parents blame the child's inability to succeed in school on his or her stubbornness or willful refusal to do better (Green 1978).

Normal childish impulses are forbidden. Infants' smiles and coos are ignored. Clean, well-fed babies are left to lie alone in their cribs for hours without being picked up, talked to, or played with. Older children's attempts to ingratiate themselves by meeting all demands and doing especially well in school are rejected. Children are subjected to days of silence or screaming. Many are saddled with heavy home responsibilities and expected to look out for their parents' welfare before their own. The maltreatment extends outside of the home when parents discourage their children from making friends among schoolmates and neighbors. Often these parents did not plan for or want the child, and fathers may refuse to help take care of the youngster (Moore 1982).

Symptoms of Emotional Abuse

It is far more difficult to identify children who are victims of emotional as compared with physical abuse. Proving that there is a real connection between parental and child behavior is next to impossible. Therefore, Garbarino and Garbarino (1980) contend that practitioners need to look for two kinds of evidence, both of which must be present before they can assume that emotional abuse has occurred. First, there should be evidence that children have "seriously impaired competence in social relationships, very low self-esteem, a consistent pattern of negative affect, and a serious inability to respond appropriately to the normal behavior of adults" (Garbarino and Garbarino 1980, 8). In addition, their parents or caretakers should be seen to reject the children, give them poor quality care, consistently disparage them, and discourage many normal childish activities.

Infants in emotionally abusive families may fail to thrive, even though they have been given adequate food and physical care. Development of speech and motor skills may be delayed. Older children, who accept their parents' evaluation of themselves without question, become life's perpetual victims, scapegoats, and losers.

Table 8-2 summarizes existing descriptions of the behavior of emotionally abused children (Broadhurst 1979; Dean 1979; Garbarino and Garbarino 1980; Garbarino and Gilliam 1980; Herbruck 1979; Moore 1982). Observation of several of these behavior may indicate that further investigation of the family is needed.

Table 8–2
Behavior Patterns of Emotionally Abused Children

Behavior Category	Age 5 and Under	Age 6 to 12
Expressiveness and apparent sense of self	Comforts self through rocking and sucking Does not play Has difficulty sleeping Is passive and compliant or aggressive and defiant Rarely smiles	Comforts self through rocking and sucking Very low self-esteem; believes self to be worthless, bad, unlovable Angry and hostile or passive and depressed May have emotional problems
Language and learning	Speech disorders or delayed language development	Speech disorders Appears driven to excel academically or shows steady decline in schoolwork and I.Q. Learning disabled
Relationships with peers	Inept social skills	Alienated; has great difficulty in making friends Lacks or has little empathy for others' feelings Becomes a scapegoat Self-destructive, sometimes antisocial behavior or withdrawn, passive behavior
Relationships with parents	Affectless and detached from parents or solicitous of them Fussy, unresponsive, irritable Watchful, yet avoids eye contact	Inappropriately adultlike behavior. Seeks to gratify parents' needs
Relationships with other adults	Relates indiscriminately to adults in charming and agreeable ways Seeks attention and always seems to want/need more	Seeks approval, attention

Patterns of Coping

Whether abuse is physical or emotional, children use similar strategies to cope with their stressful homes. Practitioners identify three typical coping patterns seen in their daily contacts with abused youngsters. McFadden (1980) has named them caretakers, hiders, and provokers. Caretakers cope by using altruism to manipulate the aggressor, hiders by withdrawing, and provokers by impulsive acting out.

Caretakers

As early as two or three years of age, children assume the caretaker role as a way of coping with their fear of repeatedly being the butt of their parents' physical or emotional abuse. Descriptions of their actions raise the question of whether this is really role reversal, since most perform their tasks without positive affect or empathy for their parents. These are not like the children of alcoholics, who freely nurture their mothers and fathers. Instead, abused children are constantly alert to adult signs of distress and physical unease. To prevent the adult's anger from boiling over, they try to be good, to keep the household running smoothly, and to do the expected thing. In the process, caretaker children deny their own wants and feelings. It becomes impossible for them to watch out for trouble and at the same time have a normal childhood.

Hiders

These youngsters try to disappear whenever there is a hint of fighting or anger. If they cannot physically leave the room, they will withdraw into themselves. They keep their distance from and mistrust adults, attracting as little notice as possible.

Provokers

Children whose impulsive acting out provokes anger from their parents, other adults, and peers have probably learned to equate punishment with love. They become adept at knowing just the one thing they can do or say that will cause an adult to physically, verbally, or emotionally attack them. They are in control of the amount, kind, and source of negative attention they receive.

    If used for any length of time, these three patterns of coping have poor prognoses. Basic to each is a pervasive inability to trust others. Children believe they are completely on their own. They cannot turn to their parents for comfort and love. They grow up in what Helfer (1976) calls the "world of abnormal rearing." Lacking trust, they become isolated individuals unable to seek or accept help. Even after these lonely children grow up and choose mates, they remain unable to develop satisfying relationships with their partners. When a child is born to them, they expect the baby to give the unconditional love and comfort they have always craved. With these unrealistic expectations of their children, Helfer contends, the cycle of abuse begins again.

Current Helping Strategies

Helfer's (1976) theory of a cycle of abuse has been widely accepted. Using its logic, one of the most effective ways to help children should be to change parental behavior to make it less harsh and more nurturant. When abuse stops, children should gain a sense of safety and begin to trust adults. Once trust is learned, the cycle of abuse should be broken. Accordingly, most efforts have been directed toward educating or rehabilitating parents.

Interventions with Parents

Social agencies involve parents in training classes and counseling, supply home visitors to model effective parenting, enroll in day care to give mothers some hours of daily respite, and assign caseworkers to guide and support family members. "Most families receive multiple therapeutic services, with a typical abusive or neglectful family receiving three services" (Starr 1979, 875). Even under these circumstances, Starr finds that practitioners are successful in preventing further abuse in less than half of their cases.

Somewhat more success has been reported by Parents Anonymous, a voluntary self-help group for adults who have abused or fear they will abuse their children. P.A.'s structure is designed to break the cycle of abuse by (1) removing parents' feelings of isolation, (2) providing friends from whom they are willing to learn, (3) increasing feelings of self-worth as members applaud attempts at improvement, and (4) building trust within the group and between members and facilitator. The organization claims that "the reported frequency of both verbally and physically abusive behavior decreases significantly as an almost immediate effect of joining P.A." (Lieber and Baker 1976, 9). Herbruck (1979) agrees that this remains a major achievement of P.A. However she points out that once the abuse stops, years of active membership are still required for parents to learn to substitute positive caretaking skills for their negative ones.

A third strategy coordinates the treatment of parents and their children. While the adults participate in group therapy, their preschoolers are in therapeutic day care. Following the adult group meeting, parents, toddlers, and program staff interact, allowing the professionals to model appropriate ways of disciplining children (Watkins and Bradbard 1982).

Star (1983) reports on an innovative program in Knoxville, Tennessee, which brings abusive families into a residential center for two weeks to learn new ways of relating to one another. For example, mothers are taught games to play with their infants that have the goal of inducing the adults to do more touching and cuddling of their babies. Parents and children receive counseling and family group sessions. When the two weeks have passed, they can request two further months of counseling. The program is too new to have been evaluated.

Certainly the most expensive parental intervention is described by Fraiberg, Adelson, and Shapiro (1975). Two skilled therapists, one a psychologist, the other a social worker, intervened with mothers and their babies in home settings under Dr. Fraiberg's superivison. They developed a strategy of "psychotherapy in the kitchen" which employed the traditional techniques of transference, repetition of the past in the present, and interpretation. To these, they added expert observations of the infants coupled with tactful education of the mothers regarding effective ways of meeting their babies' needs. In all reported cases, the adults eventually reexperienced the stress and pain of the severe abuse inflicted on them in childhood. As a result, they began to empathize with their babies and gradually incorporated the positive mothering roles which had been modeled for them by the therapists during the years of weekly contact. Mothers and children were functioning harmoniously by the end of the project.

Interventions with Children

In working with abused children, practitioners' efforts aim first at protecting them from immediate harm. Where the home is violent, they work to change parental behavior or remove youngsters and place them in shelters or foster care. However, children tend to view separation from their families as punishment; they look upon it as proof that their parents are right to label them *bad*. After all, Mom and Dad get to remain comfortably at home. The children are the ones who are forcibly uprooted. Thus, there is general agreement today that youngsters should be separated from their parents only if they are in imminent danger of severe physical or emotional injury. Even then, shelters and foster homes are expensive alternatives and provide no guarantee that the quality of care will compensate for the stress of the move.

The second goal for practitioners is to help children break the cycle of abuse. Current efforts in this direction are aimed at building trust, self-esteem, and social skills in the hope that if they have these attributes, children will grow up to provide normal parenting for their own youngsters. To date, there is no scientific evidence that these interventions have achieved this long-term goal. In the short run however, interveners report that children appear to benefit from their efforts.

Trust. Trust development is accomplished in several ways, depending on the age of the child. Day care providers encourage regression on the assumption that abused toddlers have "missed out on a dependent infant relationship with a giving mother" (Martin 1972, 111). The belief is that feeding, rocking, and holding preschoolers as though they were babies, engenders trust between youngsters and caretakers (Gardner 1975). Children learn that they can rely on the day care staff for affection, cuddling, and physical care. The development of trust is further encouraged through consistent daily routines at the center, with the same things happening in the same way day after day. Discipline is largely verbal, even with the youngest infants, and limits are set in firm but nonpunitive fashion (Bean 1975). Preschoolers are reassured that in this setting they will not be harmed.

Older children apparently have a more difficult time learning to trust adults. They engage in repeated actions to test the worker's ability to provide unconditional and consistent caring. Green (1978) suggests that it may be fruitful to allow abused children to be more dependent on the helping adult than would normally be expected. He also believes that because these youngsters are so often jealous of their relationships with caring adults, it is important to let them take home small items (a picture drawn during the session, a pencil belonging to the worker) as reminders of the adult's continuing interest.

Self-esteem. Self-esteem is nurtured in toddlers through providing day care activities at which they can be successful, staff admiration of each new accomplishment, and encouragement for the children to be proud of their achievements (Bean 1975).

Again, for older children, self-esteem develops more slowly and with greater difficulty. Teachers and social workers typically attempt to build self-esteem through a variety of individual and group human relations and values clarification exercises. Green (1978) finds it useful to remind children that abuse is more their parents' problem than their own. However, he notes that self-hatred and self-destructive behavior is often deeply ingrained by the time children reach school age.

Social Skills. Social skill development is thought to be important for abused children as a way of providing them with approval and support from outside of the family. Studies of adults find that the existence of at least one good friend can "mitigate the effects of stressful life events" (Rutter 1983, 24). It seems likely that this also holds true for children.

On the preschool level, social skill training may simply mean helping children to learn to pay attention to other people. Gardner (1975) describes a day care program for children under the age of three which emphasizes verbalization by teachers of their own feelings and those which they recognize in their pupils. Toddlers are patiently trained to be aware of their own and other children's feelings. At this age level, the ability to empathize appears to help children relate successfully with peers and adults.

In their work with older children, teachers and social workers have available a number of interpersonal skill training packages. Most of these include videotaped demonstrations of specific social skills, opportunities for children to practice the behaviors, and live or taped feedback on their performance. "In at least some cases, these programs have been notably successful in increasing the social acceptance of initially isolated children" (Rubin 1980, 58).

Proposed Helping Strategies

Looking beyond current helping strategies, there are four types of interventions that offer considerable promise, at least in theory. The first two are aimed at the control of impulsive violence and the development of empathic memory of pain. The third intervention uses the sibling group to provide nurturance within the family, and the fourth has the goal of teaching positive coping methods to substitute for the avoidance ones most commonly used by abused children. Each of these interventions has been tried by one or more clinicians or agencies working with small numbers of clients. None have been applied on a large enough scale to accommodate evaluative studies.

Control of Impulsive Violence

A major difference between abusive and nonabusive parents is that the former act out their anger toward their children, while the latter keep it under control. In recent years, sufficient evidence has been gathered to prove that family violence is repeated from one generation to the next. The reverse is also true. Youngsters who grow up in nonviolent homes habitually settle disagreements with their siblings, and later with their spouses and children, by nonviolent means (Straus, Gelles, and Steinmetz 1980). Apparently, both the expression and the control of violent impulses is learned at home.

How early does this learning take place? There is no definitive answer yet. However, after years of working with abusive parents and observing their toddlers in day care, Galdston tentatively proposes that "those children who have received significant exposure to violent behavior before the age of two are likely to have identified with this pattern of response in a fashion that proves to be essentially irreversible, although a great deal can be done subsequently to contain it" (Galdston 1979, 344).

Theoretically then, interventions with abusive families might profitably concentrate on eliminating violent behavior in the child's environment before he or she is two years old. Not only parent-child aggression, but sibling fighting, observed violence on television, and assaults in nonhome settings should probably be avoided.

Older children can be taught to contain and control their violent impulses. They can be trained to anticipate and cope with those occasional times when they explode despite their best efforts. Parents can learn impulse control through self-help groups or therapy. Obviously to break the cycle of violence, all family members need to be taught constructive methods of handling disputes.

Star (1983) reports on Kansas City's Family Training program which sends behavioral therapists into abusive homes on a weekly basis. They teach parents and children behavior modification principles and methods for reducing family conflict and avoiding violent outbursts. Between home visits, clients can phone their therapists twenty-four hours a day for help and instruction in dealing with parent-child irritations whenever they arise. Program staff claim that in three or four months they see consistent improvement in family behavior patterns.

Empathy with Pain

One of the most troubling questions about abusive parents is why they continue to inflict physical or emotional damage after it becomes evident that their children are in pain. Why doesn't the son or daughter's suffering stop the parent's behavior? One theory contends that the ability to empathize with another person's anguish develops through warm, caring home relationships. Thus, the cold, bleak childhood experiences of abusive parents have left them with an "insensitivity to the pain they cause in their victims" (Belsky 1980, 326).

Fraiberg and her associates (1975) suggest an additional explanation. In working psychoanalytically with abusive parents, they observed that these individuals had detailed memories of the horror they suffered in childhood. "What was not remembered was the associated affective experience" (Fraiberg, Adelson, and Shapiro 1975, 419). Fraiberg uses the concept of repression to explain the inability of these parents to remember their own misery and to empathize with their children's feelings. She found that once her clients reexperienced the repressed affect, they were able to stop hurting their babies.

To date there are no studies which identify the factors in the lives of abused youngsters which enable some to empathize with pain while others become completely insensitive. Clear guidelines are still needed for ways of helping children to (1) maintain the affect in memories of abuse and

(2) develop the capacity to empathize with the pain of others. However in theory at least, empathic memory for pain would be of great help in breaking the cycle of abuse.

Working with Siblings

Halperin (1981) makes a strong case for the value of working with the entire sibling group concurrently with attempts to help the parents and the abused child. She suggests that if the siblings have aligned themselves with their parents against one child, then work with the whole group can protect the scapegoated youngster. If, on the other hand, the brothers and sisters support one another, they can be assisted in making the best possible use of their love and cohesiveness to benefit their victim-member.

Bank and Kahn (1982) studied loyal sibling groups and found that while they fight among themselves, they protect their members by clearly establishing the fair limits of aggression and preventing one child from humiliating another. As they get older, they learn to use humor to deal with disputes. However, this kind of loyalty apparently does not develop in a vacuum. Somewhere in the early history of all cohesive sibling groups there is a caring adult who nurtures the youngsters. The authors go on to warn that "one cannot cherish another sibling if one has experienced profound ego impairment in the first eighteen months of life" (Bank and Kahn 1982, 124). This contention underlines Galdston's (1979) concern that interventions with abusive families occur before the maltreated youngster's second birthday.

Practitioners need to evaluate the cohesiveness of the abusive family's siblings. Under caring adult guidance, it may be possible to civilize antagonistic groups. In addition, loyal siblings can be helped to express love, offer protection from parental violence, and maintain empathy with their brothers' and sisters' feelings.

Teaching Positive Coping Strategies

A major task for professionals is to help abused children gain self-esteem and stop self-destructive behaviors. One way of accomplishing this is to teach them positive strategies which can be substituted for their existing negative methods.

Altruism. Caretaker children already use the positive approach of altruism as a defense against parental outbursts of rage. School-age youngsters ingratiate themselves with teachers and foster parents by successfully using caretaking skills. The caretaker role gives children a sense of accomplishment and control. Therefore it is probably best to encourage them to maintain and use it wherever it can be effective for their long-term development. For example, some children may be able to use altruism to their advantage in making friends with peers.

Sublimation. Green (1978) recommends that abused elementary school children be taught to use sublimation to increase their ability to cope. Practitioners can help youngsters to get involved in games, sports, and hobbies. This will enable them to make friends, to spend less time at home with their parents, and to achieve personal satisfaction and heightened self-esteem. Children may also be able to come to terms with their abusive experiences through creative activities such as writing, drawing, music, and dramatic play.

Anticipation. Anticipation is another coping strategy that can be learned by five- to twelve-year-olds. By this age, they can sense when their parents are about to attack them. They can be taught to anticipate what they will do the next time Mom or Dad threatens to explode. With an adult's help and, if possible, the parent's approval, they can plan alternate ways of insuring their own safety. For example, a child may arrange to stay with a neighbor or relative when a parent goes out of control.

Legal Issues

Today, all fifty states, American Samoa, Guam, Puerto Rico, and the Virgin Islands have enacted laws whose aim is to protect children from abuse and neglect. All require reports when a practitioner has a reason to believe that a child under the age of eighteen is being treated in a way that conforms to the particular jurisdiction's definition of abuse or neglect. Typically, teachers and other school personnel, social workers, nurses, physicians, mental health professionals, and child care staffs are mandated to report. If they fail to do so, they are subject to penalties. These range from five days to a year in jail and/or $10 to $1,000 in fines. In return, reporters are granted immunity from prosecution, even if their suspicions are not corroborated. "The majority of state laws require the agency receiving the report of abuse or neglect to initiate an investigation 'immediately,' 'promptly,' or 'within 48 hours' and to take appropriate action to protect the child" (National Center on Child Abuse and Neglect 1980, 17). Since definitions and procedures vary from state to state, practitioners need to know the specific requirements of their own jurisdictions.

Guardian Ad Litem

The majority of child abuse reporting laws provide for the appointment of a *guardian ad litem* to represent the interests of the abused or neglected youngster when a case comes to court (National Center on Child Abuse and Neglect 1980). These individuals are sometimes lawyers, but more often concerned citizens who have received special training. They function independently of both social agency and parents. Sometimes called court appointed special advocates (CASA), they can request medical or psychological tests, observe child and family interactions, interview all participants in the case, and objectively assess the facts. CASAs focus on one child at a time, and follow him or her for as many years as necessary. Thus, they provide continuity for youngsters in a system where social workers, foster parents, and even judges change from month to month. CASAs can make sure that court orders are (1) in the child's best interest, (2) carried out effectively, and (3) reviewed at reasonable intervals.

Jurisdictional Problems

Child abuse laws do not always apply to youngsters who live on Native American lands or on military bases. Because of tangled jurisdictional problems, there are children who have no legal protection against abuse. Practitioners who work in these situations need to understand the specific limits of local regulations. For example, some tribal councils protect Native American children, while others have no legal power to deal with their own juveniles. Where tribal governments do not have jurisdiction, states usually enforce their own laws (Broadhurst and Knoeller 1979).

When child abuse occurs in families living on military bases, the situation is even more complicated. If the installation has *exclusive jurisdiction,* then resident parents are subject only to military and federal laws, and these do not address child abuse at all. State reporting statutes do not apply, and "state welfare agencies cannot voluntarily initiate assistance" (Comptroller General of the U.S. 1979, 13).

On the other hand, state laws cover youngsters who live on bases where there is either *concurrent jurisdiction* (both state and military laws apply) or *partial* and *proprietary jurisdiction* (agreements enforce compliance with specific state laws). As late as 1979, military child abuse programs were poorly funded and inadequately staffed. Reporting, follow-up, and treatment procedures were judged to be "inconsistent and ineffective" (Comptroller General of the U.S. 1979, i).

Before the Adult Can Help

Work with abusive families is draining. Children and parents are so needy that the practitioner cannot possibly succeed in filling even a fraction of the identified deficits. In addition, the helper's own feelings may interfere. Some typical problems include the worker's fear of being physically harmed

unwillingness to accept his or her own anger with the client

need for emotional gratification from the client which goes unmet

need to see progress and growth in the client in order to feel competent when such growth is extremely slow

willingness to be enticed into spending personal free time with the client when the worker needs to relax and refresh

Before attempting to work with abused children, practitions are urged to form their own continuing support groups of individuals who are employed by the same agency or who serve similar families (Copans et al. 1979). Helpers are advised to seek assistance in learning to deal with their feelings and in deciding which interventions are most appropriate.

The growing number of lawsuits brought against agencies and colleagues in child abuse cases is another source of tension for protective service workers, teachers, physicians, and all other human service professionals. Legal actions are now so prevalent that the American Bar Association has issued guidelines for child welfare workers regarding their liability for failing to protect a youngster, violating a parent's rights, and mishandling foster care arrangements (Besharov 1983).

Ethical dilemmas are a third source of stress for practititoners who work with abused children. How can protection be given to all children who need it without inevitably harrassing innocent parents? How can family integrity be safeguarded and existing love preserved when outsiders interrupt almost daily to provide services? How can economic and emotional stability be restored when a parent has been forcibly removed by the court? How can a child be guaranteed higher quality psychological parenting in a foster home than he or she had in the abusive family? In the controversial book, *Before the Best Interests of the Child,* the authors argue that intervention should be restricted to cases where there is a consensus that real harm will come to the child and "about which there is a reasonable expectation that intrusion will be more beneficial than injurious to the child" (Goldstein, Freud, and Solnit 1979, 137). Most protective service workers hope to meet this standard, but realize that their definitions of the words *beneficial* and *injurious* may not match those of parents, children, courts, and colleagues.

References

Bank, S.P., and M.D. Kahn 1982. *The sibling bond.* New York: Basic Books, Inc., Publishers.

Bean, S.L. 1975. The use of specialized day care in preventing child abuse. In *Child abuse: Intervention and treatment,* ed. N.B. Ebeling and D.A. Hill. Acton, Mass.: Publishing Sciences Group, Inc.

Belsky, J. 1980. Child maltreatment: An ecological integration. *American Psychologist,* 35:320–335.

Besharov, D. 1983. *Criminal and civil liability in child welfare work: The growing trend.* Washington, D.C.: American Bar Association.

Blythe, B.J. 1983. A critique of outcome evaluation in child abuse treatment. *Child Welfare,* 62:325–335.

Broadhurst, D.D. 1979. *The educator's role in the prevention and treatment of child abuse and neglect.* National Center on Child Abuse and Neglect (OHDS)79–30172. Washington, D.C.: Government Printing Office.

Broadhurst, D.D., and J.S. Knoeller. 1979. *The role of law enforcement in the prevention and treatment of child abuse and neglect.* National Center on Child Abuse and Neglect (OHDS)79–30193. Washington, D.C.: Government Printing Office.

Comptroller General of the U.S. 1979. General Accounting Office. *Report to the Congress: Military child advocacy programs—victims of neglect.* HRD–79–75. Washington, D.C.: Government Printing Office.

Copans, S., H. Krell, J.H. Gundy, J. Rogan, and F. Field. 1979. The stresses of treating child abuse. *Children Today,* January-February.

Corrigan, J.R. 1981. Institutional abuse update. *Legal Response,* Spring.

Dean, D. 1979. Emotional abuse of children. *Children Today,* July-August.

Elmer, E., and G. Gregg. 1979. Developmental characteristics of abused children. In *Child abuse and violence,* ed. D.G. Gil. New York: AMS Press Inc.

Fraiberg, S., E. Adelson, and V. Shapiro. 1975. Ghosts in the nursery: A psychoanalytic approach to the problems of impaired infant-mother relationships. *Journal of the American Academy of Child Psychiatry,* 14:387–421.

Galdston, R. 1979. Preventing the abuse of little children. In *Child abuse and violence,* ed. D.G. Gil. New York: AMS Press Inc.

Garbarino, J., and A.C. Garbarino. 1980. *Emotional maltreatment of children.* Chicago: National Committee for Prevention of Child Abuse.

Garbarino, J., and G. Gilliam. 1980. *Understanding abusive families.* Lexington, Mass.: Lexington Books. D.C. Heath and Company.

Gardner, L. 1975. The Gilday Center: A method of intervention for child abuse. In *Child abuse: Intervention and treatment,* ed. N.B. Ebeling and D.A. Hill. Acton, Mass.: Publishing Sciences Group, Inc.

Gil, E. 1982. *Foster parenting abused children.* Chicago: National Committee for Prevention of Child Abuse.

Goldstein, J., A. Freud, and A.J. Solnit. 1979. *Before the best interests of the child.* New York: The Free Press, Macmillan Publishing Co., Inc.

Gray, E. 1983. *What have we learned about preventing child abuse? An overview of the "community and minority group action to prevent child abuse and neglect" program.* Chicago: National Committee for Prevention of Child Abuse. Mimeo.

Green, A.H. 1978. Psychiatric treatment of abused children. *Journal of the American Academy of Child Psychiatry,* 17:356:371.

Halperin. S.L. 1981. Abused and non-abused children's perceptions of their mothers, fathers and siblings: Implications for a comprehensive family treatment plan. *Family Relations,* 30:89–96.

Helfer, R.E. 1976. *Child abuse and neglect: The diagnostic process and treatment programs.* National Center on Child Abuse and Neglect. (OHD)76-30069. Washington, D.C.: Government Printing Office.

Helfer, R.E., and C.H. Kempe. 1972. The child's need for early recognition, immediate care and protection. In *Helping the battered child and his family,* ed. C.H. Kempe and R.E. Helfer. Philadelphia: J.B Lippincott Company.

Herbruck, C.C. 1979. *Breaking the cycle of child abuse.* Minneapolis: Winston Press.

Lieber, L.L., and J.M. Baker. 1976. Parents Anonymous—self-help treatment for child abusing parents: A review and an evaluation. *Frontiers,* Winter.

Martin, H. 1972. The child and his development. In *Helping the battered child and his family,* ed., C.H. Kempe and R.E. Helfer. Philadelphia: J.B. Lippincott Company.

McFadden, E.J. 1980. Fostering the battered and abused child. *Children Today,* March-April.

McPherson, K.S., and L.L. Garcia. 1983. Effects of social class and familiarity on pediatricians' responses to child abuse. *Child Welfare,* 62:387–393.

Miller, J.G. 1981. Thoughts on institutional abuse. *Legal Response,* Spring.

Moore, J.B. 1982. Project Thrive: A supportive treatment approach to the parents of children with nonorganic failure to thrive. *Child Welfare,* 61:389–399.

National Center on Child Abuse and Neglect. 1980. *Child abuse and neglect: State reporting laws.* (OHDS) 80-30265. Washington, D.C.: Government Printing Office.

————. 1981. *Study findings: National study of the incidence and severity of child abuse and neglect.* (OHDS)81-30325. Washington, D.C.: Government Printing Office.

Newberger, E.H., and J.N. Hyde. 1979. Child abuse: Principles and implications of current pediatric practice. In *Child abuse and violence,* ed. D.G. Gil. New York: AMS Press Inc.

Parents Anonymous. 1983. Evaluation report on children's program. *Frontiers,* Summer.

Rubin, Z. 1980. *Children's friendships.* Cambridge: Harvard University Press.

Rutter, M. 1983. Stress, coping, and development: Some issues and some questions. In *Stress, coping, and development in children,* ed. N. Garmezy and M. Rutter. New York: McGraw-Hill Book Company.

Star, B., 1983. *Helping the abuser: Intervening effectively in family violence.* New York: Family Service Association of America.

Starr, R.H. Jr. 1979. Child abuse. *American Psychologist,* 34:872–878.

Straus, M.A., R.J. Gelles, and S.K. Steinmetz. 1980. *Behind closed doors: Violence in the American family.* Garden City, N.Y.: Anchor Books, Doubleday.

Tooley, K.M. 1977. The young child as victim of sibling attack. *Social Casework,* 58:25–28.

Watkins, H.D., and M.R. Bradbard. 1982. Child maltreatment: An overview with suggestions for intervention and research. *Family Relations,* 31:323–333.

Neglect

Neglect is a form of child maltreatment which differs significantly from abuse in etiology and in the way in which it is experienced by the victim. Children live with caretakers who are unwilling or unable to become involved with them and who are emotionally and sometimes physically absent. As youngsters attempt to relate to these grownups, it becomes clear that their efforts have no effect. For the purposes of this book, neglect is defined as *a caretaker's indifference toward a child's basic growth needs, which results in physical, intellectual, or emotional damage to the youngster.*

The National Center on Child Abuse and Neglect (1981) documented 329,000 neglect cases in 1979–80. They reported those instances where, as a result of parental or caretaker inaction, a child's basic needs had not been met and he or she had suffered *serious* impairment or injury. Instances of moderate neglect were not included. This may account for the discrepancy between NCCAN figures and previous estimates that neglect is far more prevalent than abuse in this country (Young 1981).

Neglect occurs in many forms. It can be "chronic, periodic, or episodic" (Jenkins, Salus, and Schultze 1979). In the first instance, parents are consistently indifferent to their children's welfare. In the second, they neglect the youngsters at predictable intervals, perhaps weekends and holidays. In the third, children are neglected only when there are major accumulations of stress in their parents' lives.

Neglect varies from moderate to severe. Severely neglected children are starved, burned, accidentally poisoned, and/or injured or killed in avoidable home accidents. They live in chaos. Survivors are physically and emotionally crippled by the experience. "Children eat as they can, sleep when they must, and wander like lost souls in a world without order, without warmth, without meaning" (Young 1981, 2). In contrast, Young points out that moderately neglectful parents provide organization in at least one area of the household, give their children some warmth, and take some responsibility for them.

Jenkins, Salus, and Schultze (1979) remind practitioners that what appears to be neglect may, in some cases, be a culturally acceptable child-rearing practice in the local community. They suggest that teachers and social workers carefully observe neighborhood norms, noting whether most youngsters display the same symptoms before acting on their suspicions that a particular family is neglectful.

Ecology of Neglect

The microsystem in which neglected children live differs dramatically from accepted normal patterns, characterized by family relationships that are emotionally barren. The exosystem also is perceived as hostile by neglected youngsters; it is felt to contain enemies to be avoided rather than friends and supporters. The macrosystem further compounds the child's distress by encouraging parents to concentrate on fulfilling their own needs and by assuring adults that children are a parent's personal property, to be dealt with as they see fit.

Microsystem Dynamics

Neglectful parents share typical characteristics that impact heavily on their youngsters (Martin and Walters 1982). Many of these adults are themselves products of unstable homes, having experienced failure in school and delinquency during adolescence (Junewicz 1983). Most neglectful parents exhibit two or more of the following attributes and behaviors (Herbruck 1979; Junewicz 1983; Martin and Walters 1982; Young 1981):

  low energy level; low motivation for change

  inability to give love and emotional support to others

  unstable income resulting in recurring financial problems

  mistrust and hostility toward offers of help

  tendency to avoid problems by using alcohol, drugs, or by going to sleep for long periods

  intellectual inadequacy; mental retardation; mental illness; chronic depression

  In the most severe cases, these are families only in the biological sense. Parents may walk out of the house and stay away for days without making provision for their children's food, shelter, and safety. If they prevail on neighbors or relatives to take their children, they may not return until well after the promised date. Some mothers report forgetting about their children and not being able to hear them when they cry (Herbruck 1979). Their sons and daughters eventually stop trying to contact them.

Exosystem Factors

Neglectful families are conscious that they are outcasts in their communities. It is usual for them to withdraw from their neighbors and relatives (Hall,

DeLaCruz, and Russell 1982; Polansky et al. 1981). Because they are reluctant to allow anybody to enter their homes, they lack normal sources of
feedback and advice about housekeeping and child-rearing practices (Belsky
1980). If they are on welfare, they look at social workers as "enemies to be
evaded, tricked when possible, and mollified" (Young 1981, 2). Many fail to
take their children to doctors or clinics when they are injured or ill (National
Center on Child Abuse and Neglect 1981).

Macrosystem Pressures

Society emphasizes that parents have the right to run their homes and deal
with their children in private. This tends to reinforce the neglectful parent's
insistence on remaining isolated and beyond the reach of protective service
efforts.

In addition, Belsky (1980) points out that the current American "me
first" trend relegates the family to second place and undervalues responsible
parenting. This attitude helps to justify neglecting parents' concentration on
their own problems to the exclusion of those of their children.

Identifying Victims of Neglect

Protective service workers recognize three forms of neglect—physical, educational, and emotional. One, two, or all three can be present in a parent-
child relationship.

Physical Neglect

Researchers and practitioners uniformly describe physically neglectful
households as cluttered with garbage, piles of clothing, excrement, dirty
dishes, and stained mattresses lacking sheets and blankets. Drugs, liquor,
poisons, and matches are discarded wherever they have been used last. It is
not unusual to find a baby lying naked in a crib covered with feces and next
to it a bottle of soured milk. When the parents think to bring home food,
children must grab what they can. The adults seldom try to cook a meal and
restrict their shopping to convenience items (Herbruck 1979; Jenkins, Salus,
and Schultze 1979; Young 1981).

Parents seem unaware that they are creating stressful or dangerous situations for their children. They do not teach their youngsters to wash and
groom themselves and set no limits on their behavior. From infancy on-
wards, family members seldom talk to each other. Children remain in the
house or apartment day after day. Toddlers may never have had the experience of going outside to play or accompanying an adult to a supermarket.

Protective service workers report that when these youngsters first see other children, they don't know what to do. Typically they simply stand and look and say nothing at all. Normal children tease them for their odd behavior. When neglected youngsters go to school, their unwashed bodies smell so badly that no one wants to sit next to them. Lack of knowledge of acceptable behavior further contributes to their outcast status.

Children fare somewhat better in homes where there is moderate neglect (Young 1981). Cooked meals are served, although mealtimes are erratic. All members of the family seldom eat at the same time. The house is dirty but there is no excrement or stench. Moderately neglectful parents leave their children alone for hours rather than days. They take the youngsters to hospital emergency rooms when they are injured or very ill but pay no attention to chronic problems, such as colds and poor eyesight.

It is relatively easy to identify children who are physically neglected. For example, infants who fail to thrive often recover rapidly in the hospital, only to regress when they return home. A combination of several of the symptoms listed in table 9–1 can help to identify cases of physical neglect among school-age youngsters. Table 9–1 summarizes the findings of a number of researchers and practitioners (Jenkins, Salus, and Schultze 1979; Junewicz 1983; Young 1981).

Educational Neglect

According to the National Center on Child Abuse and Neglect (1981), large numbers of neglectful parents fail to register their children in school. Others keep their youngsters home three or more days a month to work for pay or to care for siblings. Some refuse to allow necessary remedial services for their children because the extra time spent in school embarrasses and inconveniences the parents. When teachers try to intervene, the youngsters are blamed for allowing themselves to be noticed and causing outsiders to interfere.

When educationally neglected children come to school, they "stick out like sore thumbs" because they cannot keep up academically and have difficulty relating to their peers (Junewicz 1983). Once they adapt, however, they grow in self-confidence and find security in achieving academic goals. They then begin arriving in the classroom early in the morning and staying late in the afternoon. Despite their apparent interest in school, neglected youngsters are frequently absent due to temporary parental abandonment, lack of appropriate clothing, and untreated illnesses. Some are absent so often that they are not promoted at the end of the year. Repeating a grade adds to their stress, and they may give up on school and join the truant subculture.

Table 9–1
Symptoms of Physical Neglect in School-Age Children

Physical appearance

Underweight	Dirty body and/or clothing
Frequent diarrhea	Inappropriately dressed for the weather
Tires easily	Constantly hungry; begs or steals food;
Running nose/chronic cold	rummages through garbage cans
Untended medical problems, infected wounds	

Expressiveness and apparent sense of self

Apathetic and listless	Hyperactive; uncontrolled, random behavior
Doesn't cry or laugh	
Seems to have no sense of self	

Relationships with peers

Scapegoat	Has no friends; doesn't know how to make
Outcast	friends

Relationships with parents

Doesn't turn to parents for help or comfort	Parents seem unconcerned about child; do nothing about identified problems; refuse offers of help

School behavior

Arrives early and doesn't want to go home after school	Tells teacher there is no one home to look after him or her
Comes to school tired	Doesn't play with other children
Falls asleep in class	Destroys toys; doesn't know how to play with them
Daydreams	Withdrawn and quiet or hyperactive and uncontrolled

Emotional Neglect

When parents totally ignore their children's needs for affection, attention, and emotional support, the results can be drastic, ranging from developmental delays to an older child's suicide (National Center on Child Abuse and Neglect 1981). When these youngsters reach out to their parents for love, for affirmation, or even for anger and rebuke, they are met with passive indifference (Herbruck 1979; Wald 1961). There are no rewards for being good and no punishments for being bad.

In families where there is moderate rather than severe emotional neglect, either one parent or a nearby relative cares about the children and shows them affection (Young 1981). However, this adult may not follow through with other parental responsibilities.

When the experience of emotional neglect begins at birth, it is expressed in the parents' impersonal way of touching their babies (Young 1981). As a result, infants stop crying and become unresponsive. Herbruck (1979) speculates that this lack of responsiveness creates a cycle of noninteraction between parents and youngsters which lasts throughout childhood.

By the time they enter school, emotionally neglected children don't know who they are. They don't think of themselves as good or bad or as anything at all (Herbruck 1979). When older children exhibit maladaptive behavior outside of the home or when they assault other children or their teachers, their parents do nothing (National Center on Child Abuse and Neglect 1981). If, as sometimes happens, youngsters become emotionally disturbed, these parents are likely to refuse to authorize treatment.

Emotionally neglected children may be adequately fed and dressed and receive needed medical care. It is therefore more difficult to identify them as compared with their physically neglected age-mates. Table 9–2 summarizes the findings of researchers and practitioners regarding patterns of behavior which may indicate emotional neglect (Herbruck 1979; Junewicz 1983; Wald 1961; Young 1981).

Patterns of Coping

Neglected children learn to repress pain and disappointment. Their major coping strategy is to stop feeling anything at all. In addition, they employ techniques which help them avoid stress rather than face and adapt to it.

Table 9–2
Symptoms of Emotional Neglect

Symptoms in infants

Has feeding disorders; vomits	Stimulates self by sucking, biting, scratching, rocking back and forth and banging head
Does not cry	

Symptoms in preschoolers

Indiscriminately seeks attention from anyone	Hyperactive, but actions seem to have no purpose
Has difficulty listening and concentrating	Does not cry when hurt
Has no curiosity	Does not play

Symptoms in elementary school children

Believes failure is inevitable for him or her	Acts impulsively
Is depressed, withdrawn, preoccupied with self; asocial	Has little concept of future consequences of actions
Does not cry when hurt	Seeks to escape problems
	Is defiant, rebellious, destructive, cruel
	Lies, steals

Their lifestyles fall into three categories which might be termed the losers, the hiders, and the runaways.

Losers feel powerless and doomed to failure. Fate controls them and they believe they will always be inept and unloved. A typical response is, "That's the way life is. You get used to it." Protective service workers experience losers as highly dependent.

Hiders protect themselves from stress by staying out of sight; they withdraw from contact with the world. In school hiders are quiet, affectless, and withdrawn. At home they evade the social worker's advances or are passively cooperative.

Runaways avoid stress by escaping from the situation without thought to the consequences of their actions. They rely on impulsive acting out to conceal their misery from consciousness.

Current Helping Strategies

Young (1981) contends that current treatment techniques cannot possibly work with families in which there is severe neglect. She points out that, without realizing it, parents and practitioners have opposite beliefs and purposes. The worker's goal is to help the parent and child. The parent's goal is to get rid of the outsider's pressure as quickly as possible. The result is often a stalemate. At best, the parents conform temporarily and then revert to their original practices. Young cites examples of children placed in foster homes while their parents are given training in home management and child care. When the youngsters return, their parents' reform efforts are dropped and old relationships and ways of living are resumed.

Another current practice which seems to guarantee that social workers will fail with neglecting families is the fact that caseloads are heavy and unreasonably short time limits are set on the amount of work that can be done with each family. In order to build constructive relationships with these elusive parents, professionals need to keep the same cases for several years.

School budget cuts which mandate larger elementary classes and little or no additional help for teachers also defeat efforts to break the cycle of failure for neglected youngsters. These children must be given extraordinary amounts of attention and individual tutoring before they can gain any confidence in their academic abilities. They require special help to learn how to work and play with other children and how to make and keep friends. Even one such child in a classroom of thirty children is more than most teachers can handle effectively.

Only in cases of moderate neglect do present strategies seem to succeed. When these parents come to trust a protective service worker because he or she has advocated for the adult as well as the child, they are apparently able to make some modest changes in their behavior.

Proposed Helping Strategies

Neglected children face a bleak future unless more effective techniques can be found to help them overcome their tremendous handicaps. In cases of severe neglect, Young (1981) contends that the only solution is to remove youngsters from their parents permanently. She advocates terminating parental rights and initiating adoption planning as early in the child's life as possible. She believes that severely neglectful adults cannot change themselves and cannot be helped, at least by the methods currently employed by most protective service agencies. Adoption, on the other hand, can provide a constructive environment and the necessary loving care to overcome early deficits and encourage normal child development.

Working with Parents

Psychoanalytic theory suggests that even severely neglectful parents can be helped to (1) remember, relive, and accept the pain they felt in childhood when their parents refused to love, affirm, and support them; and (2) remember, relive, and accept their losses and feelings of grief for the many times they were themselves abandoned. Fraiberg and her associates (1975) cite the case of a mother who, once she unearthed her buried feelings, suddenly was able to hug and comfort her baby. Then, with the help of a therapist who worked with her each week in her own home, she learned to empathize with the infant's separation fears and to plan for appropriate babysitters when it was necessary to leave her child for a few hours. However, weekly in-home psychotherapy takes years to produce change and is expensive compared with the cost of freeing neglected children for adoption.

One major problem in helping neglectful parents is the fact that they have never experienced more constructive lifestyles. They don't know other ways of keeping house and dealing with children. Relatively inarticulate and unimaginative, they cannot understand and introject verbal descriptions of appropriate home life. Their youngsters have never lived in clean, warm, nurturing homes. The whole family needs to experience the new lifestyle before they can attempt to copy it. Yet, to date, few agencies have been able to invent ways for neglecting parents and their children to live in surroundings where they can absorb the proposed way of living. Star (1983) reports on an experimental family camp program in Pasadena, California, which attempts to provide a complete environmental change for whole families. Within the course of a few weekends away at camp together, twelve families (1) began to trust one another and staff, (2) gained some understanding of their own destructive behavior patterns, (3) expressed love for one another, and (4) felt a sense of belonging and joy. At present, Star reports that the family camp program is no longer operating due to lack of funding.

Working with Children in School

Another strategy for breaking the cycle of neglect is to work directly with children in school settings. By helping youngsters to be successful in their studies and to develop self-esteem, teachers may be able to salvage some of these lost, directionless children. Broadhurst (1979) and Young (1981) recommend that schools offer services designed especially for neglected children. The following suggestions summarize their ideas and those of the author, based on the known developmental deficits caused by neglect.

Day care and nursery school staff need special training in the etiology of neglect so that they are prepared to give patient, unconditional care and affection to difficult children. In addition to the usual curriculum, neglected youngsters need to be taught specifically how to

play and join in playing with others; initiate play

show affection to others; accept expressions of affection

have fun, laugh, be silly

develop language and expressive skills

take care of personal hygiene

Elementary school staffs can meet the needs of neglected children through activities that can be carried out during regular school hours, with no expectation that children will do school tasks at home. Interruptions due to absences should not stop the flow of learning for individual children, and parental cooperation should be unnecessary. Components of a special program for neglected children might include

intensive tutoring to stop the cycle of failure

group sessions to develop social skills and to develop hobbies and interests which will enable children to use sublimation as a coping technique; the ability to laugh and have fun two nutritionally balanced hot meals each school day, served attractively in quiet, orderly surroundings

weekly contact with a counselor or therapist to work on acknowledging and remembering feelings and to learn new coping skills

diagnosis and treatment of chronic medical and dental problems, including provision of needed eyeglasses, dental care, hearing aids, etc.

Legal Issues

At the present time, all laws which relate to child abuse also apply to cases of neglect. The National Center on Child Abuse and Neglect (1980) maintains that since both lead to equally serious harm, efforts to distinguish between them serve no purpose. Therefore, practitioners who deal with neglected children need to know all applicable state and local child abuse reporting laws and regulations (see chapter 8).

References

Belsky, J. 1980. Child maltreatment: An ecological integration. *American Psychologist*, 35:320–335.

Broadhurst, D.D. 1979. *The educator's role in the prevention and treatment of child abuse and neglect.* National Center on Child Abuse and Neglect. (OHDS) 79–30172. Washington, D.C.: Government Printing Office.

Fraiberg, S., E. Adelson, and V. Shapiro. 1975. Ghosts in the nursery: A psychoanalytic approach to the problems of impaired infant-mother relationships. *Journal of the American Academy of Child Psychiatry*, 14:387–421.

Hall, M., A. DeLaCruz, and P. Russell. 1982. Working with neglecting families. *Children Today*, March–April.

Herbruck, C.C. 1979. *Breaking the cycle of child abuse.* Minneapolis: Winston Press.

Jenkins, J.L., M.K. Salus, and G.L. Schultze. 1979. *Child protective services: A guide for workers.* National Center on Child Abuse and Neglect (OHDS) 79–30203. Washington, D.C.: Government Printing Office.

Junewicz, W.J. 1983. A protective posture toward emotional neglect and abuse. *Child Welfare*, 62:243–252.

Martin, M.J., and J. Walters. 1982. Familial correlates of selected types of child abuse and neglect. *Journal of Marriage and the Family*, 44:267–276.

National Center on Child Abuse and Neglect. 1980. *Child abuse and neglect: State reporting laws.* (OHDS) 80–30265. Washington, D.C.: Government Printing Office.

_____ . 1981. *Study findings: National study of the incidence and severity of child abuse and neglect.* (OHDS) 81–30325. Washington, D.C.: Government Printing Office.

Polansky, N., M.A. Chalmers, E. Buttenweiser, and D.P. Williams. 1981. *Damaged parents: An anatomy of child neglect.* Chicago: University of Chicago Press.

Star, B. 1983. *Helping the abuser: Intervening effectively in family violence.* New York: Family Service Association of America.

Wald, M. 1961. *Protective services and emotional neglect.* Denver: The American Humane Association.

Young, L. 1981. *Physical child neglect.* Chicago: National Committee for Prevention of Child Abuse.

# 10

Sexual Abuse and Sexual Exploitation

Sexual maltreatment of children takes two major forms, abuse and exploitation. Both cause severe stress. If the incident of maltreatment is a one-time, nonviolent occurrence involving gentle coercion, the tension may be short-lived and the memory pushed to the back of the youngster's mind. However, many adult-child sexual relationships are repetitive and long-lasting, creating tension and guilt in the victim even when the perpetrator believes that he or she has obtained the youngster's consent. In fact, children are unable, in the eyes of the law, to give such consent. Society makes it very clear that whatever the child's behavior, adults must be responsible for acting appropriately and controlling themselves. Child victims cannot seduce offenders.

Sexual Abuse

According to the National Center on Child Abuse and Neglect (1981), there were 17,880 reports of sexually abused children under the age of twelve in the United States in 1979–80. More than 2,000 were five years old or younger. In almost half of the cases, there was evidence of oral, anal, or genital penile penetration. In addition, one-third of the sexually abused children were victims of molestation with genital contact, and eighteen percent were subjected to sexual fondling of breasts or buttocks, or exposure. Most victims were white, and eighty-three percent were girls.

Definition of Sexual Abuse

"Child sexual abuse is a sexual act imposed on a child who lacks emotional, maturational, and cognitive development" (Sgroi, Blick, and Porter 1982, 9). The key word in this definition is *imposed*, because it emphasizes the distinction between sexual abuse and normal sex-play among children of the same or similar ages. In order to identify acts which contain a potential for damage, Finkelhor (1979) defines sexual abusers as persons who are at least five years older than the targeted youngster, who are sexually more sophisticated than the child, and who are in an authority relationship to the child.

Abusive sexual acts range in severity from those where the offender has no physical contact with the child to touching and intrusion. In table 10–1

Table 10-1
Examples of Abusive Sexual Acts

No Physical Contact

Displaying genitals, undressing seductively in front of child, using adult nudity to stimulate or shock child

Openly or secretly watching child while he or she undresses, bathes, or uses the toilet

Masturbating while child watches

Having intercourse with another person while child watches

Touching

Kissing child intimately

Fondling child's breasts, belly, genitals, buttocks; requiring child to similarly fondle adult

Masturbating the child and/or requiring the child to masturbate the adult; rubbing adult genitals against child's body

Intrusion

Initiating oral-genital contact between adult and child and/or requiring child to fellate adult or perform cunnilingus

Penetrating child's anus or vagina using fingers, objects, or penis

---

examples of each kind of abuse are compiled from descriptions cited by May (1978) and Sgroi, Blick, and Porter (1982).

Incest

Much of the sexual abuse of children in the United States can be termed incest. That is, it occurs between persons who are prohibited to marry. Sex acts between a child and a parent, grandparent, aunt, uncle, or sibling are considered incestuous in all states. In addition, in some states, sexual molestation of children by steprelatives is considered incest (Browning and Boatman 1977). Researchers also report cases of multiple incestuous pairings within extended families (Bander, Fein, and Bishop 1982; Browning and Boatman 1977). That is, more than one of the children in a family may be victims of abuse, or one child may be the sexual target of several of his or her elders (Server and Janzen 1982).

The Perpetrator

In thirty percent of the cases reported to the National Center on Child Abuse and Neglect (1981), the child's stepfather was identified as the offender.

Fathers were the abusers of twenty-eight percent of the children; the mother's paramour was involved in eleven percent of the cases; and adult relatives living in the home in five percent. Mothers were identified as initiators in ten percent of the reports.

Researchers have found that perpetrators who are not members of the extended family are usually known to the child. They include friends of the family, neighbors, bus drivers, scout leaders, employers, and other who have ready access to the youngster and with whom he or she has a trusting relationship prior to the sexual incident. The abuser is a complete stranger to the victim in a minority of cases (Bander, Fein, and Bishop 1982; Finkelhor 1979).

Perpetrators' ages typically range from adolescence to the early thirties (Finkelhor 1979; May 1978). Although clinicians report instances of grandparent-grandchild incest (Forward and Buck 1978), the offender is most often a man in his twenties. Offenders are usually members of the same race as the victim (May 1978), have average intelligence, and are sane, not psychotic (Groth et al. 1978).

Those who are alcoholics or drug users commit sex offenses no more frequently when intoxicated than when sober (Groth et al. 1978). Researchers suggest that perpetrators use intoxication as an excuse for their behavior when it has, in fact, not been a factor in the incident (Finkelhor 1979).

Perpetrators tend to be unable to empathize with their victims. They do not seem to grasp that their actions are damaging to children (Server and Janzen 1982).

Motivation. Whether they are males or females, relatives or strangers, adults or adolescents, offenders have one of three basic motives. They are seeking tenderness, exercising power, or releasing sadistic rage (Bank and Kahn 1982: Forward and Buck 1978; Groth and Burgess 1977).

The perpetrator who *seeks tenderness* is gentle with the victim, slowly building a sexual relationship (Groth and Burgess 1977). The child's loyalty and acquiescence are maintained by the perpetrator's evident affection and approval and by threats that all of this will cease if their secret life together is revealed. Children are given treats, taken on trips, given gifts of clothing and toys, and singled out from their siblings for special attention. Perpetrators may have sexual or marriage partners of their own age, but they feel more at ease with children than with adults. Frequently these relationships last for several years before they are terminated. The offender usually then turns to the child's younger sibling or to another youngster who is now the same age as the victim was when their relationship began.

Perpetrators who *exercise power* over a child are sexually stimulated by the force used to overcome the youngster's resistance. They are aggressive and gain compliance by threatening, humiliating, and arousing fear, although they usually stop short of injuring the child (Groth and Burgess 1977). Often offenders have sexual partners of their own age, but feel more in control and more powerful when having sex with a girl or boy.

The perpetrator who *releases sadistic rage* through sexual attacks on children gains satisfaction by inflicting pain. Groth and Burgess (1977) contend that this small minority of offenders carefully plan their sexual assaults, stalking their victims and using weapons and beatings to force compliance. Threats of further violence insure repeated access to the child.

Female Offenders. In his retrospective study of college students' memories of childhood sexual abuse, Finkelhor (1979) found that female and male perpetrators are remarkably similar in their approaches to their victims, the kinds of sex acts they initiate, the length of time their relationships with children last, and their patterns of gentleness or use of force. However, Finkelhor found that childen are less frightened of female offenders and feel less negative about their sexual experiences with women.

Sibling Offenders. Incest between older and younger siblings follows similar patterns to those described thus far. It is most likely to occur in families where parents have abdicated their supervisory responsibilities; where children are left alone together for long periods of time; where youngsters are neglected or abandoned (Bank and Kahn 1982).

Denial after Discovery. Star (1983) contends that abusers almost always blame the victim, convincing themselves that children like the sexual activities and comply willingly. Forward and Buck (1978) cite perpetrators who deny their guilt and believe that their victim's seductive behavior caused them to lose control. In a recent study of incestuous fathers, more than half denied their culpability, even when there was clear evidence of guilt (Bander, Fein, and Bishop 1982). According to Sgroi, Blick, and Porter (1982), the perpetrator's actions are only discovered when (1) the victim decides to reveal the abuse; (2) a relative, friend, or neighbor unexpectedly comes upon the perpetrator and child engaged in a sex act; (3) a physician or nurse recognizes the cause of a child's physical injury or veneral disease; or (4) the victim's behavior alerts a teacher or social worker to the probability of sexual maltreatment.

Long-term Effects on Victims

There are apparently individuals who have reached adulthood unaffected by the sexual maltreatment which occurred when they were children (Finkelhor 1979). However, we do not know what factors in their lives enabled them to cope successfully as compared with other adults who turn to therapy for help.

Among those who seek counseling for the long-term effects of childhood sexual victimization, personality profiles contain the following characteristics

(Bank and Kahn 1982; Forward and Buck 1978; Nasjleti 1980; Sgroi, Blick, and Porter 1982):

inability to trust others

depression

poor self-concept; believing self to be ugly, impure, unworthy of love or respect; self-destructiveness

hostility; suicidal feelings; migraine headaches

poor social skills; use of seductiveness to initiate friendships

inability to get along with parents and siblings

inability to have sexually satisfying experiences with opposite sex age-mates; dislike of sex; frigidity; homosexuality; pedophilia; promiscuity or prostitution; belief that sex is the only aspect of self that is valued by others

The Ecology of Sexual Abuse

Except where otherwise specified, our discussion of the ecology of sexual abuse will concentrate on the dynamics of incestuous families, since these make up the majority of all reported cases.

Microsystem Dynamics. Abusive (step)fathers usually single out one six- to ten-year-old daughter for sexual attention. On average, they maintain the relationship for three years or until the youngster reaches adolescence (Spencer 1978). The daughter becomes her father's favorite, replacing her mother as the female authority in the household.

In these families, mothers have little affection for their husbands and children and are passive and sometimes cold or hostile, with a history of childhood sexual abuse and/or abandonment by their own parents (deYoung 1982). They may unconsciously facilitate their husband's actions by being away from home at mealtimes and when the children go to bed (Spencer 1978). They refuse to believe their daughter's reports out of fear of divorce, loss of financial support, and exposure to public scorn (deYoung 1982). Forward and Buck (1978) claim that these mothers feel so much pain at being supplanted by their daughters that they blame the girls and justify their husbands' actions.

Victims feel helpless to overcome the perpetrator's subtle coercion. They believe his assurances that they are being initiated into adult sex for their own good and see no alternative but to comply. They mistakenly believe that their mothers know about the incest and are capable of stopping it (Summit

1978). For some time, daughters hungrily bask in the warmth of their father's attention, enjoying what is, for many, the only affection they have ever known (Forward and Buck 1978). This pleasure, however, eventually adds to the child's feeling of guilt and wrongdoing (Finkelhor 1979). If her father insists on intercourse or oral-genital contact, she may experience physical pain and nausea, as well as helplessness and the sense that she has no control over her body (Forward and Buck 1978). When she discovers that she can stop the incest, she feels guilty for not having been able to terminate it when it first began. What follows is a frightening feeling of unwanted power as she realizes she can destroy her family and send her father to jail by revealing the incest secret (deYoung 1982).

The victim's siblings compound her emotional confusion. Youngsters who ache for attention and love are envious of their sister and may refuse to support her attempts to get out of the situation. They may try to curry favor with their father by actively helping him to have access to their sister (deYoung 1981). Where she has supplanted her mother, siblings may resent her inept attempts to maintain family discipline.

When incest involves a (step)father and (step)son, there is an additional emotional burden for the victim. The son may fear that he has homosexual tendencies and may resent his parent for using him in this manner.

Mother-son incest generally occurs when there is no father or other male figure in the household. Forward and Buck (1978) find that although these mothers and sons sleep in the same bed, intercourse rarely occurs. Instead, their relationship meets the mother's need for closeness and companionship. She effectively isolates her son from his age-mates by her seductiveness and demands for and appreciation of his company and attention.

Incest between older and younger siblings may start out as experimentation by the elder of the pair. It becomes an addictive form of satisfaction when the aggressor realizes that the younger sibling (as compared with non-family age-mates) makes no demands and is a readily accessible sex partner (Forward and Buck 1978). Bank and Kahn (1982) find that at the start, the victim is happy to be considered attractive and special. Later, however, when the younger child wants to terminate the activity, the elder sibling often resorts to force. Loredo (1982) finds that most parents refuse to believe the victim when he or she complains of being sexually abused by a sibling. Children feel the pain of their parents' disbelief more keenly than the hurt of the incest itself.

Exosystem Factors. The incestuous home situation always has some effect on the victim's school performance and relationships with peers. Few children are able to immerse themselves deeply enough in their studies to block out the negative effects of sexual maltreatment. For those who do, academic tasks become a haven. For the typical victim, however, school achievement declines as preoccupation with the sexual activity increases. Most have frequent absences from school for a variety of major and minor complaints. They miss essential material and fall behind in their work.

Brown (1979) points out that sexually abused girls are often their classmates' scapegoats when they seek to use their seductiveness (often the only strategy they know) to make friends with peers. Boys turn them into easy marks and then insult them. Girls consider their behavior cheap and inappropriate. If they drop the seductiveness and instead attempt to boss their classmates as they do their siblings, they are still rejected.

As a consequence, sexually abused youngsters have few, if any, of childhood's normal exosystem supports. They are inept at making friends and even when they do, there is a barrier of secrecy which remains between them and their age-mates. As one victim said, "I feel one-hundred years older than the other girls in my class."

Macrosystem Pressures. Society's strong taboo against incest has failed to protect thousands of children. Yet those who seek to remove the taboo have the potentially more damaging goal of increasing the accessibility of children as sex partners for adults. There is a small but vocal group of organizations in this country today which attempt to encourage child-adult sex. According to Rush (1980), they claim that these experiences are healthy for children. She points out however, that "today's idea of sexual liberation and the sexual freedom of children is a euphemism for sexual exploitation" (Rush 1980, 192).

Another macrosystem pressure arises from the prevalent belief that boys can't be raped. Nasjleti (1980) finds that society's contention that boys are (or should be) able to defend themselves results in the refusal of many youngsters to seek help after being sexually molested. In fact, a common attitude is that boys willingly cooperate in sex acts with their elders. If the abuser is male, the boy is considered a homosexual. If the offender is female, boys can be sure that nothing will be done to deter the perpetrator because even preadolescent males are supposed to enjoy sexual acts with older women.

Identifying Victims of Sexual Abuse

Where there are physical symptoms, the task of identifying sexual abuse victims is relatively easy. Most physicians and nurses are alert to the possibility of sexual abuse if they observe that a child's anus or genitals are bruised, swollen, or bleeding; if there is semen on the youngster's body or clothing; or if a child has a venereal disease. For example, gonorrhea infections in a

youngster's throat, urethra, rectum, or vagina definitely indicate that there
has been sexual contact.

Children whose injuries are less severe may complain of pain or itching
of genitals or anus. Sometimes they attempt to hide torn or stained under-
pants. The observer may notice that it seems painful for them to sit or take
part in sports.

According to deYoung (1982), some sexually abused children deliberately injure themselves in attempts to make themselves ugly to repel the
perpetrator or to attract the attention of someone who will stop the offender.
They may also believe they are punishing themselves for taking part in the
sex act, particularly if their bodies have responded with any degree of pleasure. When outsiders notice their injuries, however, they fail to ask for help.
Instead they invent plausible explanations for their bruises, burns, cuts, and
scratches which make them seem accidental.

If there are no physical symptoms of sexual abuse, observers may be
able to identify victims through their actions. Table 10–2 summarizes current
agreements about those behaviors which occur most often among children
who have been sexually maltreated (Adams and Fay 1981; Child Sexual
Abuse Victim Assistance Project 1979; Sgroi, Porter, and Blick 1982).

Patterns of Coping

During the months or years of sexual abuse by their (step)fathers, (step)-
daughters evolve some coping patterns which avoid and some which face
stress. Avoidance strategies generally have negative effects on these youngsters because they are used over long periods of time. Victims who regress or
withdraw, for example, cut themselves off from many of their normal opportunities for physical, emotional, and intellectual growth. Girls who use
denial often try to sleep or to imagine that they are somewhere else while
they are being assaulted. When these efforts are unsuccessful, as is usually
the case, self-esteem is undermined. Those who use impulsive acting out may
do so in the hope of signaling to an adult that they are keeping an unwanted
secret. However, most of the time their frantic efforts are misunderstood by
their mothers and teachers. Instead, they arouse the anger of the people who
they hoped would help them. In adolescence they may become promiscuous,
turn to drugs or alcohol, or attempt suicide.

Finkelhor (1979) reports that some girls who use sublimation as a coping
strategy are able to find rewards in school achievement which bolster their
self-regard. In at least one area of their lives, they feel worthy of praise.

When anticipation is the chosen coping pattern, girls are apparently able
to gain a sense of power over the aggressor (Finkelhor 1979). They plan ways

Table 10–2
Children's Behaviors Which May Indicate Sexual Abuse

Development of new fears
Fear of dark	Fear of being alone
Fear of strangers or of a specific family member, relative, friend	Fear of sleeping alone in own room
	Fear of males

Changes in usual behavior patterns
Loss of appetite	Refusal to go to favorite places or to stay with specific persons
Bedwetting	
Loss of patience; increased irritability	Sudden worry about keeping clean
Sleep disturbances; nightmares	

Overt expressions of sexuality
Precocious sexual activity; adult-like postures, e.g., mimicking mounting behavior	Excessive interest in sex; talk about sex
	Persistent sex play with toys or peers
Compulsive masturbation	Seductive behavior with peers and adults
"French" kissing	
Has more knowledge about sex than age-mates	

Changes in school performance
Stops trusting adults	Unwilling to participate in previously liked activities
Is unable to concentrate	
Sudden decline in academic performance	Hints about sexual activity; tells teacher about being afraid to go home; wants to live with teacher or in a foster home

Apparent relationships with parents
Is overprotected	Child talks seriously of running away from home
Parent seems jealous of any friends child makes outside of family	

to avoid situations in which the perpetrator might have the advantage. They stay out of his reach or turn his attention to another victim.

Legal Issues

Sexual abuse of children is a crime in all fifty states, although definitions of specific acts, ages of victims, degrees of force employed, and relationships of offenders to victims vary from one jurisdiction to another (Graves and Sgroi 1982). Physicians, teachers, social workers, and other human service professionals are mandated to report cases, but many are reluctant to do so because they know that the family will automatically become involved with the court system, sometimes with devastating results. Victims, in particular, are often traumatized by their experiences as trial witnesses. If a child's testimony is accepted, she feels responsible for sending the perpetrator to jail. If her statements are not believed, she suffers the public humiliation of being branded a liar. Human service workers also know that punishment for the offender may be a lengthy jail sentence which will deprive the family not only of a financial provider, but of a member who, under less harsh circumstances, might be helped to change his ways.

There is currently considerable support for legal reform to protect victims without violating the civil rights of defendants (Ordway 1983). One of the proposed reforms is a procedure for having the child's testimony taken by an expert interviewer in a quiet, private setting. This professional, who is experienced in handling cases of child sexual abuse, asks the youngster questions provided by the defense and prosecution attorneys and records the answers. The recording is presented in court by the adult who is then available for cross-examination regarding the victim's competency and credibility (Ordway 1983). Another reform, which is in effect in several states, provides treatment facilities rather than jail for offenders, allowing them to retain their jobs and continue to support their families while living in approved residences and participating in rehabilitation programs (Star 1983).

Despite flaws in the judicial system, sexual abuse cases must always be reported to the police. Experienced practitioners maintain that too many perpetrators give only lip service to therapeutic interventions unless they are under sentence. Without the element of forced compliance, many drop out of therapy as soon as the sessions begin to demand acceptance of guilt and evidence of real behavior change (Forward and Buck 1978).

Graves and Sgroi (1982) contend that victim and offender are best served when helping professionals work on sexual abuse investigations cooperatively with the police. They urge practitioners to learn how to assist law enforcement officials in gathering evidence through physical examination of the victim, saving stained clothing, obtaining photographs, and so forth. Sometimes the knowledge that there is such data available to the court is sufficient to influence the perpetrator to acknowledge his culpability. If the child must appear in court, they suggest that his or her therapist and the police work together to prepare the youngster for the experience. They warn that it is difficult to be fair to both adult and child, in other words, "to protect the rights of the accused and to insure the safety of the victim" (Graves and Sgroi 1982, 328).

Interviewing Sexually Abused Children

All investigations begin with the gathering of information about the abuse from every available source. An interview with the victim, if he or she is three years of age or older, is essential. Sgroi, Porter, and Blick (1982) find that investigative interviewing of young children is a skill that can be learned through training and practice. The younger the child, the more expertise is required. They maintain that carefully conducted interviews not only produce accurate information, but also serve as the child's first opportunity to begin to come to terms with his or her experience. Therefore, they believe that interviewers should have clinical as well as investigative skills.

Building Rapport. The first step in interviewing sexual abuse victms is to build rapport between interviewer and child. Holder and Mohr (1980) suggest a gentle but businesslike approach in which the adult explains who he or she is, why the child is being interviewed, what background the interviewer has in this kind of work, and that he or she has talked with other children who are like the victim.

Small furniture that is comfortable for the youngster and a quiet, private room in a neutral setting outside of the child's home are other essential components. Zwerdling (1974) emphasizes the importance of using the same room, the same toys, and the same interviewer for each meeting when several sessions are needed for information-gathering. She warns adults to be helpful and sympathetic, but to carefully avoid aligning themselves with the child against other adults. A youngster who is uncomfortable about being alone with the interviewer can choose to be accompanied by an adult he or she trusts. Obviously, this should be someone other than the youngster's parents. The child's ally should be asked to remain silent and to sit near the youngster but out of his or her view. In that way the ally provides support but doesn't influence the child's responses (Sgroi, Porter, and Blick 1982).

Gathering Information. Once rapport has been established, the interviewer is advised to let the victim tell his or her own story without interruptions, letting any silences remain until the child fills them (Zwerdling 1974). The interviewer can then go over the story again, using drawings, anatomically correct dolls, and other necessary props to help insure that the adult understands exactly what the child means to convey. The interviewer should use the child's own words once their meaning is clear, rather than attempt to teach him or her adult terms (Holder and Mohr 1980). Burgess, Holmstrom, and McCausland (1978) suggest that the adult have dolls, puppets, and a play hospital and dollhouse available when working with preschoolers. Six- to twelve-year-olds can be expected to respond more readily to action toys, art supplies, and table games, with the anatomical dolls or puppets only used to clarify details in their descriptions of the abuse.

In addition to problems with vocabulary for describing genitalia and sex acts, children have difficulty estimating time spans and pinpointing dates. Sgroi, Porter, and Blick (1982) establish time sequences by asking youngsters to link sexual episodes with other significant events in their lives such as birthdays, holidays, and special school or family occasions.

During the interview, the adult needs to observe the child's body language, moods, and other evidence of his or her feelings, and include these in the record of the interview. Several breaks should be taken for fun activities which allow the child to deny his or her pain for a time and to engage in genuine play (Zwerdling 1974). Even with a break or two for recreation, children will often change the subject when interview material becomes too painful. Sgroi, Porter, and Blick (1982) suggest that the adult allow the diverson for a time and then gently return to the topic when the youngster appears able to do so. Sometimes the interview session will have to be terminated at this point and taken up again a day or two later. In fact, it is often useful to plan for two or more interviews to recheck facts and fill in blanks.

Over the series of meetings, the investigator must find out

what happened

how long each incident lasted

where it took place

where other family members were at the time

exactly when each episode occurred

over how long a period the sexual relationship existed

whether anybody else in or outside of the family knew about the abuse

why the child complied with the abuser

why the youngster is now telling about the sexual abuse (Sgroi, Porter, and Blick 1982)

Relationship Between Interviewer and Child. Zwerdling (1974) reminds interviewers that they must be sure that any reassurances they give children are realistic. Holder and Mohr (1980) reiterate that it is dangerous to make any promises to youngsters at this stage before attempts have been made to change the family situation. They remind practitioners to avoid blaming the victim's parents. The interviewer is not a surrogate parent; he or she is not a source of love. The authors warn that it is important for the adult to avoid any sexual overtones in his or her relationship with the youngster. If the child tries to be seductive, he or she must be gently but firmly stopped. Practitioners are referred to Sgroi's *Handbook of Clinical Intervention in Child Sexual Abuse* for detailed discussions of interviewing techniques.

Current Helping Strategies

There are currently four major helping strategies in cases of sexual child abuse. One form of intervention is aimed only at victims, another only at perpetrators. A third type of program involves the entire family in cooperation with the court. The fourth strategy is one of prevention through public education and consciousness-raising. Most organized efforts to prevent sexual abuse and to heal victims and their families have been in existence for only a few years. Because they are so new, research on their efficacy is meagre. Even communication among practitioners working in the field is limited. Star (1983) identifies one of the reasons for this sense of isolation among professionals. She notes that a thirty percent cut in the budget of the National Center on Child Abuse and Neglect eliminated helpful countrywide demonstration projects and forced the agency to "withdraw the special attention previously given to sexual child abuse" (Star 1983, 59).

Interventions with Victims. Most experts believe that it is best to work with the victim and the family at the same time. Thus, interventions designed specifically for children are generally used in conjunction with efforts to reform the perpetrator and to strengthen the ability of the family to support the child.

The first goal of any treatment program for victims is to provide for their safety. Three factors are necessary to insure that the youngster will not be maltreated again (Server and Janzen 1982; Spencer 1978):

The perpetrator must admit guilt and agree to stop the molestation and/or be physically separated from the victim so that further abuse becomes impossible.

The victim must demonstrate his or her ability to report further instances of sexual maltreatment immediately.

The child's caretakers must show their determination to protect him or her in the future.

Next on many victims' lists of priorities is a private, gentle medical examination to find out if there has been any physical damage to his or her body. Porter, Blick, and Sgroi (1982) find that young girls in particular believe that something is broken inside of them if there was any pain during the sexual episode. Venereal disease discovered by the examination can be treated. Most of all, the child needs reassurance that he or she has a healthy body and will be able to live a normal life.

Table 10–3
Ways to Help Children Cope with the Aftermath of Sexual Abuse

Source of Stress	Ways to Help Children Cope
Feeling that he or she is alone; fear that nobody will believe what has happened	Reassure child that adult is glad child can tell about the abuse and believes the child. Adult is sympathetic and sorry about what has happened.
Fear of beng sent away from home; being vulnerable to further abuse	Together explore reality of fears. Help child find an ally who can be trusted to help in the future. Explain arrangements that have been made to protect the child.
Guilt for complying with abuse	Emphasize reality; child was not responsible for initiating or continuing the relationship.
Guilt for causing family disruption by exposing abuse	Emphasize reality; child is not responsible for what has been happening since exposure.
Guilt for having treated siblings poorly while he or she was the favored child	Help child acknowledge and accept responsibility for his or her behavior; help child learn to relate better with siblings.
Anger, rage at perpetrator	Help child learn to express anger in constructive ways.
Self-hate, depression, suicidal thoughts	Therapy is indicated. Group therapy has helped some children cope with these feelings.
Confusion about new role in family; how to go back to being a child again	When at least one family member helps the child, this role change can be accomplished fairly easily. Otherwise, role-playing and/or counseling may help.
Feeling that he or she will always be a victim and will always be under another's control	Help child learn to make choices and decisions for him or herself; learn to be assertive.

Table 10–3 summarizes some additional ways to help children cope with the aftermath of sexual abuse (Adams and Fay 1981; Porter, Blick, and Sgroi 1982).

Existing organized programs for sexually abused children emphasize counseling, art therapy, and/or self-help groups. An example of a self-help group is Daughters and Sons United, based in California. On a nationwide level, Parents Anonymous has recently established a Children Helping Children program. Youngsters work with professionals to develop activities through which peers can help one another come to terms with their experiences of sexual abuse.

Most programs begin individual therapy or counseling with victims as soon as the abuse is revealed and continue until the youngster is strong enough to work on mutual problems with his or her siblings and parents. Toys, puppets, and art activities are used with preschoolers who are unable to express their feelings verbally. Therapists aim to build trust and self-esteem and to give youngsters a consistent experience of relating to an adult who is concerned for their security and safety. Some counselors use role-playing with young victims to aid them in understanding their own feelings and to give them opportunities to practice new behaviors.

Naitove (1982) describes an art therapy program for traumatized children using an "artmobile" in which the therapist brings materials directly to the victims' homes. The art experience helps youngsters to ventilate and come to accept their negative feelings. It also seems to remove barriers to normal intellectual and social development.

Interventions with Abusers. Few perpetrators volunteer for treatment. In order to work effectively with these resistant individuals, Sgroi (1982) believes that the practitioner must be convinced of two facts: (1) that the planned treatment will be effective and (2) that it is ethical to force these clients to take part in their own rehabilitation. She contends that until practitioners learn to work successfully with involuntary clients, the rate of recidivism will continue to be high.

Washington state's Sex Offender program is an example of an intervention designed for resistant offenders. Star (1983) describes the involvement of participants in peer therapy for as many as thirty hours a week, using modeling and social learning theory to effect change. The attitude of the men that children are sex objects is considered to be a learned disorder which can be remedied through intensive training. For example, the men are taught that they will have to exert strict control over their contacts with children for the rest of their lives. They learn to give up sexual fantasies about children and to develop imaginary scenarios in which they are sexually involved with women their own age. In operation since 1965, the goal of this carefully designed, authoritatively run program is to safely return participants to the community after three or four years.

Interventions with Families. The pattern in most family treatment programs is to start with individual therapy for each member before bringing pairs together to examine their relationships. Involvement of the family as a whole is usually the last step in the process. This pattern is followed in incest cases (which make up the majority of the clients served by all established programs), and it is also used when an outsider has assaulted a son or daughter.

The oldest family treatment program in the country was established by Giarretto for Santa Clara County in California in 1971. In its first twelve years, more than thirty-five hundred sexually abused children and their families were helped, using methods based on the behavior change theories of humanistic psychology (Giarretto 1983). Right from the start, and including the period of the perpetrator's incarceration, there is individual, mother-daughter, father-daughter, and family counseling. If parents and children decide their goal is to be reunited, marriage counseling is included. In addition, each person becomes part of a peer group (Daughters and Sons United or Parents United) which helps him or her to acknowledge interpersonal inadequacies and experiment with healthy new behaviors. The family also learns to use community resources to solve problems such as unemployment, inadequate housing, legal entanglements, debts, and need for medical services.

Giarretto's Child Sexual Abuse Treatment program serves as a model for others around the country, as well as a training experience for practitioners. Staff members work together to prevent individual burnout and to support one another in gaining skill and accepting their own limitations (Summit 1978).

Connecticut's Sexual Trauma Treatment program is an example of a successful demonstration whose National Center on Child Abuse and Neglect funding was terminated by budget cuts. The staff used the authority of the courts to bring families into the program. Once enrolled, at least two therapists were assigned to each case. Their goal was to make it impossible for the family to repeat old ways of interacting. Among the techniques used were individual therapy to build trust, art therapy to overcome resistance, group therapy to change denial into acceptance, and family and marital therapy to rebuild relationships between spouses and among parents and children. A police officer, a prosecutor, an internist, and a lawyer met regularly with the therapists to keep them in touch with the family's exosystem problems.

The Sexual Trauma Treatment program was unique in that it employed a team of evaluators to assess its effectiveness from inception to termination. By the end of the program, the majority of victims were able to return home in safety and ninety percent had an adult ally to help them in case of further abuse. On the debit side, in more than half of the cases, the perpetrator and child could no longer live in the same household. In addition, families tended to stop therapy if court charges against the offender were dropped (Bander, Fein, and Bishop 1982).

An example of a third family treatment approach is Massachusetts' Norfolk County Juvenile Diversion program. Stetson (1981) reports that the program only accepts cases when both parents openly acknowledge that they are to blame for the incestuous situation and that their child was in no way responsible. If the parents do not accept blame, then the perpetrator is prosecuted.

When the family enters treatment, the offender, usually the child's father or stepfather, remains at home unless his spouse requests his removal or the staff judges the mother unable to control her husband and protect her daughter or son. Program staff refer accepted families to outside agencies or private practitioners for counseling, but maintain supervision throughout the course of the treatment. One counselor works with the parents as a couple. His or her first task is to obtain their agreement to a behavior contract which stipulates that they will attend counseling sessions regularly, never repeat the abusive behavior, take responsibility for their children's healthy growth, and avoid making the victim a family scapegoat (i.e., not blame him or her for the family's present situation). The counselor determines how long the contract needs to be in place. If it is broken, the perpetrator is prosecuted.

In the Juvenile Diversion program, children remain in their own homes. They receive intensive individual counseling. There are also sessions with their siblings in order to create a support system. Stetson reports that youngsters learn new behaviors more rapidly than their parents, usually completing the treatment process six months before their elders.

Preventive Education. Since 1980, a steady stream of books, films, and educational programs have been published to fill the needs of schools and community agencies interested in preventing sexual maltreatment of children. The authors of these materials believe that even the youngest children can be taught to distinguish between nurturant and sexual touching. Theoretically, once a child can make this distinction, he or she can also learn how to avoid abuse. For example, the Kansas Committee for the Prevention of Child Abuse has developed a dramatic presentation for children called "Bubbylonian Encounter" which demonstrates the difference between positive touching and forced sexual touch.

Special materials for handicapped youngsters aim to reduce their risk of being sexually abused. Many mentally retarded, blind, deaf, and physically disabled youngsters lack the sophistication that might enable them to recognize when they are being led into a sexually abusive situation. To remedy this, the staff of the Minnesota Program for Victims of Sexual Assault has developed a curriculum for handicapped children that uses assertiveness training and role-playing to teach youngsters to identify "negative touching" (O'Day 1983).

Adams and Fay (1981) have compiled detailed instructions for adults who are concerned with helping children to identify and avoid situations in which sexual abuse might occur. In addition to learning to recognize sexual touch, they suggest that youngsters be taught to

trust their feelings of discomfort and tell an adult ally right away about uncomfortable incidents

believe that they have the right to control who touches them

refuse to comply if they don't understand an adult's request back out of and report to their ally all situations where (1) they are asked to do something they don't understand, (2) they are threatened with retribution if they don't do something, and (3) they are offered bribes for doing something or not telling about something.

Sexual Exploitation

Sexually exploited children are youngsters who are used by adults to

pose for pornographic films, photographs, and videotapes or take part in pornographic performances

become members of groups of children who together meet the sexual demands of one or more adults

work as prostitutes

Little public attention has been paid to the problem of child sexual exploitation. Existing data come from clinicians working with youngsters who have turned to them for help; from detectives assigned to investigate exploitation cases; and from a small number of researchers. As a result, the findings reported in the remainder of this chapter must be considered to be tentative.

Exploitative activities are apparently conducted on several levels, ranging from a father who takes seductive photographs of his son or daughter to organized crime syndicates which produce pornography and supply customers with child prostitutes. At the first level, the perpetrator may use the photographs as a way to introduce his son or daughter to sexual acts later to be repeated in partnership with the adult. Or the pictures may be an end in themselves—a way of communicating with other adults who trade or purchase such materials. At the other end of the spectrum is the child prostitution industry operated for profit by organized crime syndicates. According to Burgess (1981a), syndicates protect their computer lists of customers with elaborate codes. They maintain toll-free telephone numbers which clients can use to request specific children (usually boys) chosen from catalogs of photographs.

Midway between these two extremes are what Burgess and her associates (1981) term *child sex rings*. These consist of one or more adults who gather a group of children to regularly pose for pornographic pictures and/or take part in sex acts. The youngsters know one another and often entice siblings and friends to join them. The activities take place in motel rooms or in the adult's home and usually continue for several years. Summit (1981) describes one ring organized by a sixth grade teacher which included at least twenty-five boys over a period of eight years.

The children are paid for their services with affection, money, trips, clothes, cigarettes, liquor, drugs, and special privileges such as being allowed to drive the adult's car. Their compliance is further enforced by threats of physical violence, of losing the adult's affection, and especially of losing their place in the cohesive group of peers (Burgess et al. 1981). Ring members are aware that the perpetrator watches them carefully and is alert for any attempted disloyalty (Burgess 1981b).

Characteristics of Perpetrators

Male perpetrators predominate and, while some are parents or relatives of their victims, the majority of reported cases involve adults who are known to the children but are not family members.

Summit (1981) claims that many perpetrators are predatory adults who have a basic need to exploit children but who are expert at hiding behind a facade of complete respectability. Many are married. Often they are trusted members of the community, for example, teachers, scout leaders, professional men, and good neighbors. When one of these individuals is exposed as the organizer of a child sex ring, local parents (even parents of victims) respond with disbelief and suspicion that the children who have reported his behavior are deliberately trying to cause trouble for the adult.

Characteristics of Victims

Child sex rings often contain mixed groups of boys and girls of varying ages from six to twelve. What little is known of their family backgrounds suggests that they come from every socioeconomic level and from intact as well as chaotic homes.

During their years of membership in the ring, children experience intense conflicts between feelings of loyalty to their parents and to the offender. In some cases, the latter is their only source of consistent attention and affection. Yet they know that what they are doing is wrong and worry about keeping secrets from their families. The longer the situation continues, the more guilty they feel, and the harder it becomes to tell about their experiences and break out of the ring.

Meanwhile, the perpetrator teaches the children that what they are doing is morally right and that their parents' values are old-fashioned and wrong. Summit (1981) finds that youngsters come to value the material comforts the perpetrator supplies and to feel superior to their "straight" classmates. They look down on children who lack the spending money and privileges they enjoy and who do not share the excitement of their secret, illegal lives. Some feel contemptuous of naive helping professionals who are unaware of the existence of this sexual underworld.

Eventually some children learn that they can control the perpetrator by withholding their favors until they get specific rewards. Youngsters become manipulative and begin to think of themselves as omnipotent. They have learned to be expert sexual partners but at the same time derive little pleasure from their bodies. They separate sex from emotion in much the same fashion as adult prostitutes (Burgess et al. 1981; Knecht 1981; Schoettle 1980).

Retrospective data collected from thirty-six victims and their parents after the exposure of six sex rings, revealed physical, emotional, and intellectual symptoms similar to those of sexually abused children (Burgess et al. 1981). Coping patterns used while the rings were in existence included withdrawal from school and religious activities, impulsive acting out (including stealing and fighting with peers), and actions which hinted at sexual abuse (e.g., drawing genitals on pictures in books and magazines, acting seductively with peers).

The Aftermath of Sexual Exploitation

Child sex rings come to the attention of the authorities in a number of ways. Sometimes children tell their friends or parents. Neighbors of the perpetrator or local police may become suspicious and investigate. In any event, exposure often results in additional stress for the victims. Youngsters and their families report being harrassed by neighbors to the point where they feel impelled to move out of their homes (Schoettle 1980). Children are required to recount their experiences in detail to their parents, police officers, social workers, and defense and prosecution attorneys. These adults often refuse to believe that a "nice guy" like the offender could possibly have committed the acts described by the children (Burgess et al. 1981; Schoettle 1980). Parents blame themselves for not having known what was going on and for having failed to protect their youngsters. While they rage at the perpetrator, they also blame their sons and daughters (Burgess et al 1981; Summit 1981) for

involving their siblings in the ring

choosing to participate in the ring

not telling their parents immediately

exposing their parents to shame and ridicule

Knecht (1981) reports three cases in which the victims, all of whom were female, had nightmares about their impending court appearances. All felt dumb and scared because they had been a part of a sex ring. They were manipulative in their relationships with adults. The three girls had become used to smoking marijuana in the ring and to having all the clothes and toys they wanted. When these were no longer available, they turned to stealing and shoplifting.

Helping Children Cope with the Aftermath of Sexual Exploitation

There is no help routinely furnished to children who have been members of sex rings. Sometimes the only therapy they receive is the contact they have with a detective who takes their initial testimony and guides them through their court appearances (Knecht 1981). Parents, and children as well, often want to put the experience behind them as soon as possible and to forget it (Summit 1981).

Schoettle (1980) reports one case of a girl who voluntarily sought therapy for her feelings of helplessness and depression. The youngster first was helped to express a flood of conflicting emotions of relief and fear. After the period of catharsis, therapist and child worked to rebuild her relationship with her parents. Gradually this victim learned to accept her own strengths and weaknesses. Normal growth and development resumed when she had effectively learned "nonsexual ways of communicating and receiving affection from peers, family, and other adults" (Schoettle 1980, 296).

Legal Issues

In 1978 Congress passed the Protection of Children Against Sexual Exploitation Act which prohibits the transportation of children across state lines "for the purpose of sexual exploitation," and allows the federal government to prosecute people who produce or sell child pornography (Nash 1981, 2). In addition, this legislation extends to boys as well as girls the protection of the Mann Act, which defines sexual activity between an adult and a child under twelve as statutory rape. All but two states have supplemented the federal legislation with their own laws. Most label specific forms of sexual exploitation of children as felonies and impose penalties ranging from one year to life in prison and $1,000 to $50,000 in fines.

Practitioners may find that their state's laws ignore the harm done to the exploited child and focus instead on the issue of whether or not the film, videotape, photograph, or sexual performance is obscene. In fact, according to Nash (1981), existing legislation does not provide for the treatment of victims. He points out, however, that helping professionals may be able to define cases as coming under the protection of state child abuse statutes and thus secure funding and services needed to help the youngster.

References

Adams, C., and J. Fay. 1981. *No more secrets: Protecting your child from sexual assault.* San Luis Obispo, Calif.: Impact Publishers.

Bander, K.W., E. Fein, and G. Bishop. 1982. Evaluation of child-sexual-abuse programs. In *Handbook of clinical intervention in child sexual abuse,* ed. S.M. Sgroi. Lexington, Mass.: Lexington Books, D.C. Heath and Company.

Bank, S.P., and M.D. Kahn. 1982. *The sibling bond.* New York: Basic Books, Inc., Publishers.

Brown, S. 1979. Clinical illustrations of the sexual misuse of girls. *Child Welfare,* 58:435-442.

Browning, D.H., and B. Boatman. 1977. Incest: Children at risk. *American Journal of Psychiatry,* 134:69-72.

Burgess, A.W. 1981a. Child victim services: Spectrum of child victimization. Paper presented at conference, Second Annual Seminar on Sexual Assault. Massachusetts Criminal Justice Training Council, Brookline, Mass., January 6.

————. 1981b. The use of children in pornography and sex rings. *Legal Response,* Summer.

Burgess, A.W., A.N. Groth, and M.P. McCausland. 1981. Child sex initiation rings. *American Journal of Orthopsychiatry.* 51:110-119.

Burgess, A.W., L.L. Holmstrom, and M.P. McCausland. 1978. Counseling young victims and their families. In *Sexual assault of children and adolescents,* ed. A.W. Burgess, A.N. Groth, L.L. Holmstrom, S.M. Sgroi. Lexington, Mass.: D.C. Heath and Company.

Child Sexual Abuse Victim Assistance Project. 1979. *A message to parents about: Child sexual abuse.* Washington, D.C.: Children's Hospital National Medical Center.

deYoung, M. 1981. Siblings of Oedipus: Brothers and sisters of incest victims. *Child Welfare,* 60:561-568.

————. 1982. Self-injurious behavior in incest victims: A research note. *Child Welfare,* 61:577-584.

Finkelhor, D. 1979. *Sexually victimized children.* New York: The Free Press, Macmillan Publishing Co., Inc.

Forward, S., and C. Buck. 1978. *Betrayal of innocence: Incest and its devastation.* New York: Penguin Books.

Giarretto, H. 1983. *Integrated treatment of child sexual abuse: A treatment and training manual.* Palo Alto, Calif.: Science and Behavior Books.

Graves, P.A., and S.M. Sgroi. 1982. Law enforcement and child sexual abuse. In *Handbook of clinical intervention in child sexual abuse,* ed. S.M. Sgroi. Lexington, Mass.: Lexington Books, D.C. Heath and Company.

Groth, A.N., and A.W. Burgess. 1977. Motivational intent in the sexual assault of children. *Criminal Justice and Behavior,* 4:253–264.

Groth, A.N., A.W. Burgess, H.J. Birnbaum, and T.S. Gary. 1978. A study of the child molester: Myths and realities. *Journal of the American Criminal Justice Association,* 41:17–22.

Holder, W.M., and C. Mohr, eds. 1980. *Helping in child protective services: A casework handbook.* Englewood, Co.: The American Humane Association.

Knecht, R. 1981. Impact on child and family. Paper presented at conference, Child victimization, pornography and prostitution. Boston University School of Nursing, Boston, March 12.

Loredo, C.M. 1982. Sibling incest. In *Handbook of clinical intervention in child sexual abuse,* ed. S.M. Sgroi. Lexington, Mass.: Lexington Books, D.C. Heath and Company.

May, G. 1978. *Understanding sexual child abuse, Volume 1.* Chicago: National Committee for Prevention of Child Abuse.

Naitove, C.E. 1982. Arts therapy with sexually abused children. In *Handbook of clinical intervention in child sexual abuse,* ed. S.M. Sgroi. Lexington, Mass.: Lexington Books, D.C. Heath and Company.

Nash, D. 1981. Legal issues related to child pornography. *Legal Response,* Summer.

Nasjleti, M. 1980. Suffering in silence: The male incest victim. *Child Welfare,* 59:269–275.

National Center on Child Abuse and Neglect. 1981. *Study findings: National study of the incidence and severity of child abuse and neglect.* (OHDS)81–30325. Washington, D.C.: Government Printing Office.

O'Day, B. 1983. *Preventing sexual abuse of persons with disabilities: A curriculum for hearing impaired, physically disabled, blind and mentally retarded students.* Sexual Abuse Education for Disabled Adolescents Project. St. Paul: Minnesota State Documents Center.

Ordway, D.P. 1983. Reforming judicial procedures for handling parent-child incest. *Child Welfare,* 62:68–75.

Porter, F.S., L.C. Blick, and S.M. Sgroi. 1982. Treatment of the sexually abused child. In *Handbook of clinical intervention in child sexual abuse*, ed. S.M. Sgroi. Lexington, Mass.: Lexington Books, D.C. Heath and Company.

Rush, F. 1980. *The best kept secret: Sexual abuse of children*. New York: McGraw–Hill Book Company.

Schoettle, U.C. 1980. Child exploitation: A study of child pornography. *Journal of the American Academy of Child Psychiatry*, 19:289–299.

Server, J.C., and C. Janzen. 1982. Contraindications to reconstitution of sexually abusive families. *Child Welfare*, 61:279–288.

Sgroi, S.M. 1982. Family treatment. In *Handbook of clinical intervention in child sexual abuse*, ed. S.M. Sgroi. Lexington, Mass.: Lexington Books, D.C. Heath and Company.

Sgroi, S.M., L.C. Blick, and F.S. Porter. 1982. A conceptual framework for child sexual abuse. In *Handbook of clinical intervention in child sexual abuse*, ed. S.M. Sgroi. Lexington, Mass.: Lexington Books, D.C. Heath and Company.

Sgroi, S.M., F.S. Porter, and L.C. Blick. 1982. Validation of child sexual abuse. In *Handbook of clinical intervention in child sexual abuse*, ed. S.M. Sgroi. Lexington, Mass.: Lexington Books, D.C. Heath and Company.

Spencer, J. 1978. Father-daughter incest: A clinical view from the corrections field. *Child Welfare*, 57:581–590.

Star, B. 1983. *Helping the abuser: Intervening effectively in family violence*. New York: Family Service Association of America.

Stetson, R.B. 1981. Treatment of incestuous families. Paper presented at conference, Second Annual Seminar on Sexual Assault. Massachusetts Criminal Justice Training Council, Brookline, Mass., January 6.

Summit, R. 1978. Sexual child abuse, the psychotherapist, and the team concept. In *Dealing with sexual child abuse, Volume 2*, ed. J. Ensminger, V.J. Fontana, B.G. Fraser, and R. Summit. Chicago: National Committee for Prevention of Child Abuse.

————. 1981. Barriers to recognition and treatment of sexual abuse. Paper presented at conference, Child victimization, pornography and prostitution. Boston University School of Nursing, Boston, March 12.

Zwerdling, E. 1974. *The ABCs of casework with children: A social work teacher's notebook*. New York: Child Welfare League of America, Inc.

11 Child Victims of Parental Alcoholism

The most widespread cause of severe stress for school-age children in the United States today is life with an alcoholic parent. Estimates of the number of these children range from twelve million (Deutsch, DiCicco, and Mills 1982) to twenty-eight million (Grauer 1980). Deutsch and his colleagues estimate that "in any given classroom in the country it may be assumed that 4 to 6 of every 25 children come from alcoholic homes" (Deutsch, DiCicco, and Mills 1982, 148).

In the early 1970s it was usually the father who was the family alcoholic. However, with the rate of alcoholism rising among women and particularly among employed married women, it is almost as likely that children will have alcoholic mothers as drunken fathers (National Institute on Alcohol Abuse and Alcoholism 1981).

Despite the fact that each family has its individual expectations, there are typical sets of unreasonable demands on all children of alcoholics. The same patterns have been found in families at every socioeconomic level and in every racial, religious, and ethnic group.

The first demand is secrecy. Family members are expected to keep the alcoholic's behavior to themselves. No matter how it confuses or scares them, children are expected to maintain to outsiders that their parents are nice, sober people.

The second demand is that children take responsibility for their alcoholic parents. That may mean flattering and diverting a drunken father to save a younger sibling from a beating, staying home from school to watch over a stuporous mother, or making excuses to a parent's employer.

The third demand is that the child's own feelings be neither acknowledged nor expressed. Much of the time the alcoholic and the sober spouse are incapable of empathizing with the needs of their children. One is absorbed in getting the next drink and the other is trying to walk the tightrope of their marriage. Promises made to children on Wednesdays will not be kept on Fridays because a bout with booze will interfere, and the children's resulting anger and disappointment will go unnoticed.

The fourth demand is that children accept the blame for their parent's drinking. A mother may say, "If you hadn't been late getting home from school, I would never have needed to take that drink." The parents, on the other hand, are allowed to blame their own misbehavior on the effects of alcohol. They typically tell their children, "I said that because I was drunk. I don't remember it."

The fifth demand is that at least one child in the family become a substitute for the alcoholic spouse. This child is maneuvered into providing the sober spouse with emotional support, being a confidant and companion, and taking over household chores and repairs.

Each of these demands produces stress for the child. The combination, is, in itself, a definition of severe stress, yet millions of children each year somehow learn to cope with all five demands.

Patterns of Coping

There is no data at present to describe how infants, toddlers, and preschoolers experience life with an alcoholic or what coping methods they adopt. Recently, however, several attempts have been made to categorize the techniques that five- to twelve-year-olds have evolved for coping with their parent's demands (Ackerman 1978; Black 1979; Byrne 1980). These authors have grouped the wide range of children's strategies into distinctive clusters. As yet, no research has been done to test these categories. Also untested is the widely held belief that most children's coping styles eventually become self-defeating. However, a survey of current research points to recurring patterns of depression and alcoholism as these youngsters enter late adolescence (Deutsch, DiCicco, and Mills 1982).

Superkid or the Responsible One

Called superkid by Byrne (1980) and the responsible one by Black (1979), this child's pattern of coping is to conform to the sober parent's demand for a substitute spouse. "The role most typical for an only child, or the eldest child in a family, is one of being responsible, not only for him or herself, but for other siblings and/or parent(s)." (Black 1979, 24). Even at a tender age, superkid shoulders housekeeping and child care tasks and still gets good grades in school. This is true role reversal, with a child voluntarily becoming a parent to the adults. Relatives and friends of the family admire superkid and believe that this child has made an adjustment to life that is mature and praiseworthy (Byrne 1980). To them, superkid seems to float through a disastrous home life without a scar. But, by using altruism as his or her exclusive coping strategy, superkid has swallowed years of anger and resentment, made no close peer friendships, and never really experienced childhood. Byrne claims that as an adult, superkid tends to go to one of two extremes. He or she may become an alcoholic or marry an alcoholic and raise another superkid. At the other end of the spectrum, with the advantage of having done well in school and having learned to be altruistic, superkid may enter a service career and make a significant contribution to the profession (Byrne 1980).

Extrapolating from this description, it is possible to cluster superkid's coping methods into healthy and self-destructive patterns.

Healthy Patterns	*Self-destructive Patterns*
Takes responsibility and cares for others; puts others' needs before his or her own; behavior is prosocial.	Is unable to recognize and assert own needs and feelings, particularly feelings of anger and resentment.
Skillfully manipulates and controls siblings' and parents' behavior.	Has deep need to continue to control and manipulate others' lives.
Does well in school.	Seems unable to be light-hearted, egocentric, irresponsible, dependent, or even naughty (i.e., childlike).
Has learned home management skills.	

The Placater

Some youngsters with innate social skills work hard to keep things running smoothly at home. Black (1979) calls them placaters. They have evolved a form of altruism aimed at pleasing their parents. Placaters are seen by Mom and Dad and outsiders as sensitive people who are strong and comforting and who listen well. Placaters have little time to be children as it continually necessary for them to monitor their parents' moods and seek ways to make them feel good. Placaters' coping patterns persist into adulthood, with spouse and children being placated while personal needs are pushed into the background. When the placater's family grows up and the children leave home, or if the marriage fails, alcohol may be chosen to fill the void.

As with superkid, an examination of the placter's constellation of coping methods shows that some are healthy and some are self-destructive.

Healthy Patterns	*Self-destructive Patterns*
Is sensitive to others' moods.	Has a compulsive need to be continually alert to others' moods, and to adapt own behavior to please others.
Is sociable and adept at helping others to adjust and feel comfortable.	
Is a good listener.	Is unable to recognize and assert own needs and feelings, particularly feelings of anger and resentment.
	Has little sense of self-worth.

The Adjuster

The adjuster learns to be flexible and to subjugate his or her needs to those of the alcoholic parent and sober spouse (Black 1979). Happily jumping into

Dad's car to go for a swim on a hot day, the adjuster is willing to sit in the automobile and wait patiently for hours while Dad stops at a bar to quench his thirst on the way to the pool. Adjusters use a form of altruism to cope with the stresses of living with an alcoholic parent. In adulthood, adjusters usually allow themselves to be dominated by others and often have little self-esteem or self-confidence. Many find their adult lives have more meaning and direction when they set up housekeeping with an alcoholic mate.

An analysis of adjuster's coping patterns shows only one that is healthy, while two are likely to be self-destructive.

Healthy Patterns	Self-destructive Patterns
Is able to be flexible and to adapt to others' needs and interests.	Is unable to recognize and assert own needs and feelings, particularly feelings of anger and resentment.
	Has little sense of self-worth or self-confidence.

Alkykid

Alkykid identifies with the alcoholic parent (Byrne 1980). He or she observes that the alcoholic's needs are frequently met by others and that every pain and sorrow can be drowned in a stiff drink. Alkykid learns to manipulate adults and his or her peer group using techniques copied from the alcoholic. Teachers quickly identify alkykid as one who uses the coping strategy of impulsive acting out. He or she is a troublemaker, a potential delinquent, and is often written off as a lost cause. In early adolescence, alkykid begins to drink to solve problems. Before reaching adulthood, he or she has usually become an alcoholic.

Observers instinctively label alkykids as losers because so many of their coping patterns have negative consequences. Even alkykid's two healthy adaptations can turn sour without exceptional luck or expert guidance from a concerned adult.

Healthy Patterns	Self-destructive Patterns
Is able to manipulate others to take care of his or her needs.	Has little sense of self-worth and little self-control.
Is able to express anger and resentment.	Acts dependent and demanding, evoking anger or disinterest from others.
	Insists on quick and easy solutions to problems; has low frustration tolerance.
	Does poorly in school.

The Have Child

In his book *Children of Alcoholics: A Guidebook for Educators, Therapists, and Parents,* Ackerman (1978) categorizes the children of alcoholics in a way that is quite different from the descriptions of Byrne (1980) and Black (1979). He postulates that the children of alcoholics are either haves or have nots. "What they have or do not have is an ability within themselves to establish positive primary relationships outside the home" (Ackerman 1979, 21). Ackerman states that constructive coping lies in children's capacities to bond with or make lasting attachments to adults who are not family members, yet who care deeply for them in return.

Have nots are unable to make these bonds. Corresponding roughly to Byrne's alkykid, "many studies show that children in the 'have not' category exhibit such problems as delinquency, anxiety, and depression" (Ackerman 1979, 21).

Haves seek and accept nurturance from adults other than their parents. When a have is lucky enough to find an adult who is willing to be consistently available to him, the relationship neutralizes the trauma of living with an alcoholic. The child has a safe place to disappear to when violence threatens; somewhere to seek and receive comfort; an adult who will treat him or her like a child. Haves appreciate the substitute parent, often maintaining the relationship long into adulthood.

Examination of Ackerman's description leads to the conclusion that the have child has only one complex, healthy coping pattern.

Healthy Patterns	*Self-destructive Patterns*
Is able to establish a positive primary relationship outside the home, leading to a normal childhood with a part-time surrogate parent.	None

Identifying Children Who Need Help

The prognosis for children growing up in alcoholic families is bleak. These children are twice as likely to develop an alcohol problem as children of abstainers and moderate drinkers (National Institute on Alcohol Abuse and Alcoholism 1981). It is therefore important to identify them as early as possible and to help them modify their coping techniques to emphasize healthy patterns.

It is difficult to be certain that a child is the son or daughter of an alcoholic without knowing the family intimately. However, youngsters give clues through their appearance and the amount of nurturing they seem to receive, their school performance, their ability to make friends, and some of the things they say and do.

Appearance and Evidence of Nurturing

Some alcoholic parents nurture in brief bursts so that their children appear to outsiders to be fine for short periods and neglected the rest of the time. A youngster who is clean and sensibly dressed some mornings and disheveled on others may be the product of an alcoholic home. Other identifiers include coming to school or to the community center visibly ill; needing dental or medical care but getting it only sporadically; bringing a good lunch to school some days and no lunch at all on others.

School Performance

When children's grades take a sudden dip, when they seem incapable of producing any homework, and when they begin to get into fights, a home problem is indicated. In alcoholic families these behaviors may cure themselves as suddenly as they started and then recur after a period of days or weeks. Teachers report that some children of alcoholics perform more poorly on certain days of the week or at specific times of day. "Many children who are concerned about going home may perform well all day and then do poorly or lose attentiveness during the last class of the day" (Ackerman 1978, 71).

Children of alcoholics frequently break appointments with counselors and teachers because their parent's erratic demands must be met first and their own obligations come second. School attendance records are spotty; they are good for several weeks and then irregular with absences that do not follow the usual pattern for an illness.

In schools which run alcohol education programs, administrators report that it is relatively easy to spot the children of alcoholics. A student who is usually active and involved may become silent and withdrawn during the lesson on alcohol. A quiet child may turn into a lively participant. Others hang around after the lesson so they can be alone with the teacher (Deutsch, DiCicco, and Mills 1982). The teacher who then listens without making judgments about the youngster or his or her parents may be told about the alcoholic home.

A more subtle clue can lie in a child's complete lack of understanding that people can drink without becoming drunk. Deutsch (1978) finds that these children believe that adults drink only in order to get drunk. Thus, when the class discussion turns to levels of appropriate drinking at parties, they may insist that abstinence is the only alternative since they have never seen their parents able to take one drink and stop.

Teachers are often the first to be told, quite indirectly, that a parent is an alcoholic, and the parent does the telling. These mothers and fathers make their problems known by failing to keep appointments, showing up for meetings smelling of liquor, or offering the home visitor a beer at ten o'clock in the morning. Braun reports that they make phone calls at odd hours about subjects which have nothing to do with their child's school work. "One teacher was called at 7:00 p.m. Saturday night because the mother noticed that her linen had been stolen off the clothes line" (Braun 1980, 6).

Ability to Make Friends

Children of alcoholics are reluctant to develop close friendships or to bring classmates home after school because they are afraid their parents will be drunk. Many are isolates or loners. There are cases, of course, where peers actually know that a child's parent is a drunk and where they make the youngster the butt of their teasing and taunting.

The Things Children Say and Do

Nursery school children who have alcoholic parents are likely to bring this to the teacher's attention by talking about alcohol or acting as though they were drunk. In the group play of three-, four-, and five-year-olds, Braun observes that "Mention of bottles, poison and bars or falling to the floor and imitating a weaving walk are invitations children offer to talk about booze" (Braun 1980, 6). When asked directly about what is going on at home, they spill out their stories.

Older children are more protective. They maintain that their home lives are normal and serene; that Mom couldn't come to open school night because she had a cold; that Dad didn't make it either because he was out of town.

Current Helping Strategies

Alcoholic parents have many avenues of assistance open to them, including Alcoholics Anonymous for the drinker, Al-Anon for the sober spouse, and a variety of federal, state, and private therapy options. Most treatment concentrates on parents in the belief that if alcoholics can be cured, then life for their children will automatically improve. The fallacy of this assumption is that "there is a period of years before the parents may be healthy role models. We cannot rely on parents to undo the emotional damage to their children. They are not apt to recognize any problems when the children outwardly appear fine. Yet the children have developed and are using a very sophisticated denial system and certainly need an ongoing recovery program—as much as the parent—to get well" (Black 1979, 27). Unfortunately, according to the National Institute on Alcohol Abuse and Alcoholism (1981), only five percent of the children of alcoholics receive assistance in learning to cope.

Some alcoholism counselors believe that children can best be helped when the work is done in cooperation with their parents and siblings. Wegscheider (1981) points out that the coping strategies these youngsters have evolved are so bound up in their parents' and siblings' complex interactions that they need to be reshaped in the context of the changes other family members are making. She describes an ideal model for treatment based on Satir's philosophy of family therapy. It begins with residential or outpatient care for the alcoholic, accompanied by individual and peer counseling for spouse and children. This is followed by group sessions with the family as a whole. Later, several sets of parents and children meet together to continue their efforts to build healthy family systems.

In contrast to the family therapy approach, many programs are founded on the assumption that "children can be helped to understand their feelings and change their behavior within and outside of the family, whether or not parents are involved in treatment" (Deutsch, DiCicco, and Mills 1982, 155). Such interventions are aimed at youngsters age six and older and are located mainly in schools and community multiservice centers. Their goals are generally educational (to teach about alcoholism to help children understand their reactions to the alcoholic) and social (to help youngsters reshape their own behavior, make new friends, have fun).

Because of the alcoholic family's compulsive need for secrecy, it is sometimes difficult to recruit children and maintain their attendance without recriminations from parents. As a result, some projects offer "incentives, enticements, and excuses, both in order to attract children initially and to enable them to keep coming in safety" (Deutsch, DiCicco, and Mills 1982, 160). Once in the program, children work in peer groups, usually for relatively short periods of time, perhaps once or twice a week for four to ten weeks.

School curricula geared generally to all children, not just those who have alcoholic parents, are usually presented in a series of brief lessons. Children's groups are led by specially trained teachers, social workers, psychologists, and lay people, although some programs are experimenting with peer leadership. One community agency, CASPAR, in Somerville, Massachusetts, trains teenagers to work with younger children (Deutsch, DiCicco, and Mills 1982).

No longitudinal studies have been done on graduates of these children's programs. However, Deutsch and his colleagues (1982) report that administrators, staff members, and child participants believe there has been change for the better in such areas as school achievement, personal hygiene and health care, acting-out behavior, and ability to make friends. These authors cite one program which claims that in half of their cases, youngsters have also influenced their alcoholic parents to come in for counseling.

Proposed Helping Strategies

It is proposed that in addition to the current practice of working with groups of children, concerned adults examine the ways in which individuals cope and design interventions to support positive behavior and encourage change only where the child is clearly harming himself. In accomplishing this, practitioners need to consider the kinds of help which children need in all areas of their lives, within and outside of their families.

Helping Children Live with Their Families

Attachment to a caretaker in the first few years of life is apparently crucial to the child's later ability to cope with a chaotic household. Thus, when there is an infant in an alcoholic home and neither parent is emotionally able to provide consistent care, it may be important to arrange for outside care for at least a part of each day. If a secure bond was established in the years before the parent became an alcoholic, then the five- to twelve-year-old may only need help in continuing to love his or her parents despite the changes that alcohol has made in their relationship.

Most children feel that they should be able to do something to stop a parent's drinking. They spend endless hours finding and emptying hidden liquor bottles and trying to keep the parent away from booze. Byrne (1980) believes that practitioners can absolve the children's sense of guilt by showing them that it is impossible to rescue their parents. It is also helpful for many youngsters to understand that alcoholism is a disease. Parental behavior becomes less intimidating when children know about memory blackouts, impaired thinking, neglect of food, tremors, etc. As parents stop drinking, children need to recognize withdrawal symptoms, and as sobriety is reached, they need to appreciate how difficult it is for the parent to be a teetotaler. Excellent books written especially for children are available in public libraries and can be used to answer their questions.

Older children can learn to discount a mother or father's defensive behavior. Armed with this insight, they can cope with irrational reactions to their report cards, athletic performance, choice of friends, and taste in music.

Preteens find it helpful to know that "some alcoholic parents know they are hurt-ing their children, but they don't know how to stop themselves" (Hornik 1974, 8).

Children of alcoholics need to know how to protect themselves from the drunken parent's aggression. "Approximately 50 percent of the children we see witness or experience violence related to drinking in the home" (Black 1979, 27). They need places to retreat to that are safe and things to do that are absorbing enough to take their minds off parental shouting matches and battering. One elementary school teacher helped a girl in her third grade class to pack a small travel bag with a nightgown, toothbrush, and favorite toy so that she would have the courage to go upstairs to a neighbor's apart-ment when her parents began to fight (O'Sullivan 1976).

Until recently, practitioners have encouraged children to refuse to take responsibility for younger brothers and sisters in order to force the alcoholic to see how deficient he or she has been in carrying out parental duties. No one knows the long-term effect on children of virtually abandoning their siblings in order to teach their parents a lesson. But there is new data to suggest that taking care of younger siblings leads to self-confidence and a healthy sense of power. Werner and Smith's (1982) study shows that taking care of younger brothers and sisters correlates with an older child's ability to be resilient in difficult situations. It is not clear how the care of younger siblings contributes to resilience, but one possible interpretation is that as older children see their siblings growing up under their care and achieving well, they feel a kind of self-affirmation.

Helping Children Live with Themselves

As we have seen, denial of feelings is a typical coping strategy for children of alcoholics. It helps them adapt to their parent's inability to offer comfort and protects them from disappointment and pain. Over a lifetime, however, denial can lead to loneliness, depression, and despair. Breaking through the self-protective shell of denial is a slow, delicate process. Before a child can acknowledge repressed feelings the youngster must be in a situation where he or she feels secure. Group sessions with other children of alcoholics seem to offer an environment that leads slowly to the ability to give up at least part of the denial system (Black 1979). Most group leaders design structured ses-sions which contrast dramatically with the children's unstructured homes and serve snacks to emphasize the nurturing role of the group. They involve children in skits so they can act out some of the "awful stuff" that happens at home. Art work, puppets, films, and games are used to encourage expression of feeling. The children know that nothing they reveal will be passed along to their parents.

Once a child has gained the ability to identify feelings, he or she needs help in expressing these emotions in contained and constructive ways. Byrne

(1980) finds it important to teach a whole repertoire of tension breakers and ways to express anger. She encourages children to jog, scream, punch pillows, shoot baskets, and write about their experiences of rage.

Children of alcoholics experience so many surprises and disappointments that they may come to believe that their lives are ruled by others and that they have no control, even over their own actions. An honest evaluation of a youngster's achievements in each area of life (school, sports, homemaking, caring for siblings, hobbies) may help the child to recognize that he or she has already accomplished many things.

The fear of becoming an alcoholic themselves remains in the back of these children's minds. Deutsch (1978) observes that even though they swear they will never drink, most eventually do, experiencing a lot of guilt in the process. He recommends that concerned adults teach children sensible drinking patterns while they are still young in order to help them face the coming peer pressures against abstention as they enter their teens.

Children of alcoholics may not know how to search for solutions to their problems. Their parents cope with frustration by getting drunk. So older boys and girls may substitute marijuana for liquor, without recognizing that drugs and alcohol are two sides of the same coin (Byrne 1980). These young people have not lived in families where a mishap becomes an adventure or where the whole family has fun figuring out a new way to play a game. They need adults to help them to learn to think of alternatives and to realize that they can find many ways to solve problems.

Helping Children Thrive in School

Daily school attendance makes it easier for children to achieve at the top of their potential, develop peer friendships, and forget family turmoil for a while. Teachers can prevent an alkykid from fighting and becoming the class clown. Adjuster and placater can be encouraged to be more assertive. Even as superkid's "too good to be true" behavior is appreciated, he or she can be encouraged to be more childlike. Sensitive teachers make themselves available as willing listeners; they are open to talking over problems and to helping children find alternatives. They have the courage to talk about alcoholism when children bring up the subject.

Superkid, adjuster, and placater are good listeners and sensitive to others' moods. They know how to make adults feel comfortable, and need only a little help from their teachers to transfer these assets to relationships with peers. All benefit from opportunities to have fun and to enjoy mischief and jokes. If they feel that these youngsters need to develop more social skills, teachers can locate and use any one of a number of packaged programs to help them. These are designed to teach children the steps in making friends, how to settle arguments, how to handle jealousy, and how to deal with ethical dilemmas.

Before the Adult Can Help

Before they can help the children of alcoholics, adults need to understand their own reasons for using or rejecting alcohol. They must be honest about personal reactions to drunks. Feelings of anger and disgust will block the helper's effectiveness in appreciating how a child can adore as well as fear an alcoholic parent (Byrne 1980).

Deutsch and his colleagues (1982) emphasize the importance of participating in a thorough training program, lasting at least eight and preferably more than twenty hours, before practitioners begin working with children. Trained helpers are able to react quickly in emergencies and to help children cope on a daily basis. They know (1) the causes of alcoholism; (2) the symptoms of each stage; (3) the symptoms of sudden withdrawal; (4) typical family reactions when sobriety cannot be maintained; (5) current research on treatments for alcoholics and their children; and (6) the locations, costs, and range of services available for children and parents in the local community.

For as long as they work with children, helpers need to be constantly aware of their roles as outsiders rather than members of the family. Neither superparents nor rescuers, they must remain objective adults, disengaged from the family's interrelationships and focused on the children's needs (Byrne 1980).

Finally, the potential helper must recognize that there will be youngsters who cannot successfully be brought back to health. Some have been damaged irrevocably. Some need the services of a trained therapist over a period of years. The family may build a solid wall against the outside world and refuse assistance. There may be a personality mismatch between the helper and the child or there simply may not be enough time to build the trust relationship that is essential before growth can begin.

Legal Issues

If practitioners suspect that alcoholic parents abuse or neglect their children, they are mandated by law in all fifty states to report the case promptly. In a few states, the fact that a child living with an alcoholic is in danger of physical harm—even though he or she has not yet been abused—may be grounds for legal action. These states require that either two or three criteria be met before they will act on behalf of the youngster. New York, Nebraska, Iowa, and Rhode Island require that (1) the parent be an alcohol user who is habitually drunk and (2) that the parent's use of alcohol poses a threat or danger to the child. Wisconsin, Illinois, and California insist on the two criteria listed above and add a third, that the child have already been removed from his or her parent's custody for a year or more (Grauer 1980).

Another issue for helpers relates to maternal alcoholism prior to a baby's birth. This is a new concern in most states and there are, as yet, no definitive laws. However, the problem of maternal alcoholism as a form of child maltreatment prior to birth is growing in size and severity. "In the United States in 1977, chronic alcoholic mothers gave birth to 6,000 babies with what has become known as 'fetal alcohol syndrome' " (Grauer 1980, 8). These infants were born mentally retarded, with poor motor development, low birth weight, and a cluster of characteristic facial abnormalities.

Several states have ruled that a child born addicted to heroin is a "dependent or neglected" child. It seems likely that in the near future, similar decisions will be made regarding fetal alcohol syndrome infants. "In the light of society's increasing interest in protecting the health of unborn children, and in the light of the known adverse effects of alcohol on the fetus, it seems possible that forcible state intervention on behalf of the unborn child of an alcoholic mother may eventually become a reality" (Grauer 1980, 10).

References

Ackerman, R.J. 1978. *Children of alcoholics: A guidebook for educators, therapists, and parents.* Holmes Beach, Fla.: Learning Publications, Inc.

Black, C. 1979. Children of alcoholics. *Alcohol Health and Research World,* 4:23–27.

Braun, S.J. 1980. Some family matters that affect young children. *BAEYC Reports,* 22:3–10.

Byrne, M. 1980. Helping children to cope with alcoholic parents. Presentation at conference, Helping children to cope with stress. Lesley College, Cambridge, Mass., January.

Deutsch, C. 1978. Reaching children from families with alcoholism: Some innovative techniques. Paper presented at annual meeting of Alcohol and Drug Problems Association of North America, Seattle, September.

Deutsch, C., L. DiCicco, and D.J. Mills. 1982. Services for children of alcoholic parents. In *Prevention, intervention and treatment: Concerns and models.* Alcohol and Health Monograph no. 3. National Institute on Alcohol Abuse and Alcoholism (ADM) 82-1192. Washington, D.C.: Government Printing Office.

Grauer, N. 1980. Alcoholism and child maltreatment: Correlations and legal applications. *Legal Response,* March-April.

Hornik, E.L. 1974. *You and your alcoholic parents.* Public Affairs Pamphlet no. 506. New York: Public Affairs Committee.

National Institute on Alcohol Abuse and Alcoholism. 1981. *Alcohol and health.* Fourth special report to the U.S. Congress from the Secretary of Health and Human Services. (ADM) 81–1080. Washington, D.C.: Government Printing Office.

O'Sullivan, R. 1976. Helping children cope with their alcoholic parents. Presentation at conference, Children of alcoholic parents: The teacher's role. Lesley College, Cambridge, Mass., January.

Wegscheider, S. 1981. *Another chance: Hope and health for the alcoholic family.* Palo Alto, Calif.: Science and Behavior Books, Inc.

Werner, E.E., and R.S. Smith. 1982. *Vulnerable but invincible: A longitudinal study of resilient children and youth.* New York: McGraw-Hill Book Company.

12 Helping Strategies for Nontherapists

In the backgrounds of children who are good copers are caretakers who have supplied them with an essential growth ingredient which Bronfenbrenner (1976) calls an "enduring, irrational commitment." We have seen that these criticially important elders are usually, but not always, parents. Other adults and older siblings can effectively provide unconditional love and acceptance. Werner and Smith (1982) have shown that networks of relatives and friends can give youngsters this basic affirmation and support.

In addition to love, good copers have had the experience of facing and overcoming pain and stress (Chandler 1982). They have learned to be hopeful in the face of adversity. They know they will be able to find solutions to problems.

Therefore, in addition to the many recommendations in the preceding chapters of this book, it is suggested that adults help children to cope with stress in two important ways. One is to teach them how to make friends with their peers, neighbors, and others in the community so that they have many people with whom they share affection and who will support them when they are having difficulties. The second strategy is to ensure that youngsters develop sturdy feelings of competence based on their success in identifying and dealing with many different kinds of stress. As they anticipate stressful situations, they can also learn to choose effective coping techniques.

Teaching Children How to Make Friends

Even one warm extrafamily relationship with an adult or a peer can help immeasurably in coping with stress (Rutter 1983). Having someone to turn to, whether for comfort or for a chance to deny or suppress anxious feelings for a few hours, can provide support and strength.

In addition, friends help children learn how to get along in social situations. They are central to youngsters' concepts of who they are and what they can do successfully. Friends function as mirrors to help children establish their identities. Although some parents push their sons and daughters to be popular, studies indicate that the quality of existing friendships is more important to children's mental health than the number of people with whom they associate (Rubin 1980). Apparently, some children

165

Table 12-1
Characteristics of Popular Children

Sensitivity to Others

Quickly becomes aware of the behavior, speech, and appearance norms of any group he or she enters.

Is attentive to verbal and nonverbal feedback about own behavior.

Is neither hypersensitive nor insensitive.

Understands how others feel; is empathic.

Praises others realistically; is tactful.

Expressiveness

Displays a range of emotions.

Expresses ideas enthusiastically.

Makes positive remarks about others.

Shows affection.

Is funny, fun to be with; laughs easily; shows enjoyment of activities.

Interaction Patterns

Responds readily when invited to play or talk.

Pays attention to others, listens, and responds.

Is pleasantly assertive.

Plays or works steadily; allows others to decide when to end the activity.

Takes turns; shares graciously.

Offers help and encouragement.

Cognitive Skill

Is able to foresee consequences of actions.

Has lots of ideas for things to do.

Can manage conflict and repair ruptured friendships.

---

attract and need many friends, while others can live happily with only one or two close relationships.

Characteristics of Popular Children

Observations of popular children help practitioners define the specific friend-making skills that can be taught to less able youngsters. Table 12-1 lists a range of characteristics common to popular children, as observed by the author and by Oden (1982), Rubin (1980), and Stocking, Arezzo, and Leavitt (1980). Of course, no individual has all of the attributes described, but the list can identify areas in which isolated children may need help.

Children's Concepts of Friendship

Boys and girls who live in chronically stressful homes often have had few opportunities to observe and practice the complex process of making friends. This skill, which seems to come so easily to the average youngster, eludes them. Usually they lack a group of specific interpersonal capabilities.

One such deficit may be that the friend-making technique they employ is drastically unsophisticated compared with the methods used by their agemates. Selman and Selman (1979) have outlined a sequence of stages which they believe children go through in understanding the meaning of friendship and thus in initiating and building relationships. These stages are conceived of as overlapping one another, and each is incorporated into the next higher level rather than discarded.

The stage 0 youngster, age three to seven years, chooses friends because of the way they look, their proximity, and their material possessions.

The four- to nine-year-old stage 1 child believes that friends are people who do what you want them to do.

In stage 2, six- to twelve-year-olds consider individuals friends if they agree to play the same game or work on the same project together. When partners disagree, the friendship is at an end.

By stage 3, which generally begins around age nine and continues into adolescence, children are able to work with other people in more mutually satisfying ways. They can accept that their friends have different points of view and that they can argue and still remain close.

A few children under the age of twelve reach stage 4, in which they realize that even their dearest friends need to develop and grow in their own ways. They accept the fact that sometimes relationships must change character in order to accommodate one or both of the partners.

The Selmans urge practitioners to observe children carefully to identify their stages of functioning before attempting to plan ways to help them reach more age-appropriate levels. Most youngsters will need to move gradually from their present point through each intervening stage before reaching the level of their age-mates.

Packaged Training Programs

For generations teachers have helped children to develop social as well as academic skills. They have made it possible for outcasts to become accepted members of their classes. In the process, they have been aware that as relationships with peers and teachers improved, so did other areas of the children's lives.

In recent years, special packages have been designed and marketed to assist teachers and counselors in developing children's social skills. These generally begin with a period of diagnosis of the child's difficulties. This is followed by filmed, videotaped, or live demonstrations of needed skills. Then there is time for study and practice during which the youngster receives feedback on his or her performance. Finally there is some form of test of the child's new capabilities (Stocking, Arezzo, and Leavitt 1980). Rubin (1980) points out that the fact that youngsters can do well in a role-play test may not mean that they can actually use these abilities in everyday life. Several project directors have taken this factor into account in making their evaluations and have used independent observers to rate children's skills in natural settings without knowing which youngsters had received training. Under these rigorous conditions, evaluations two to six weeks following the end of a training project find consistent increases in social effectiveness. Some researchers report gains lasting a year or more.

A common element in the packaged programs which report the most long-lasting results is their reliance on a one-to-one relationship between a child and an adult during the practice and feedback period. As we have seen in the previous chapters, many stressed children need an adult's exclusive attention in order to learn. Once they have such a relationship, however, they are able to concentrate and move forward.

The following descriptions represent a sampling of available programs rather than a complete catalog, because new materials are published each year. The references at the end of the chapter indicate sources of detailed information about specific packages.

Starting Friendships, Acting Positively, and Managing Conflict. In their book *Helping Kids Make Friends,* Stocking, Arezzo, and Leavitt (1980) outline a three-part procedure that can be used by concerned adults to help children learn to initiate friendships, act in positive ways with others, and manage conflicts. Practitioners are urged to start by discovering a child's specific deficits in interpersonal relationships. Careful observation can pick out those behaviors which alienate other people. Further study will show how well-liked youngsters respond in similar situations. Armed with this information, the adult can then provide demonstrations which illustrate effective ways of relating. The youngster practices these skills through role-playing, first with the adult, and then with peers. The authors suggest that this be done in brief daily sessions lasting perhaps five or ten minutes.

Immediate feedback should be given so the child learns how to correct mistakes and build on successes. They suggest rewarding children with praise, hugs, smiles, and particularly with statements which describe the effective actions the child has taken. Correction of ineffective behavior should be done as gently as possible. Above all, the authors urge patience. Learning to make friends takes a great deal of time and support from an adult. In addition, the authors believe that because this person functions as a role model, he or she needs to practice what he or she preaches.

Joining a Group, Cooperating, Communicating. The technique of coaching described by Cartledge and Milburn (1980) proves to be an effective way to help children learn how to join in playing a game, how to take turns and share materials, and how to express ideas, listen to others, and offer help and encouragement. Oden (1982) found that the coaching procedure enabled children who were classroom isolates to make statistically significant gains in status rankings among their peers after taking part in only five brief sessions over a period of four weeks.

Coaching usually begins with an adult giving a child a five- to seven-minute verbal description of effective ways to get started playing a game, to take turns and share, to communicate, and to offer the other player(s) support and praise. The child is then asked to respond with examples of how each tecnique would make it more fun to play with other children. Immediately afterward, the youngster plays a game for ten minutes with a partner who is a moderately popular member of his or her school class. When the game is over, the target child and the coach talk about the new techniques that were used and how effective they were in action. The procedure is repeated at least four more times over the next few weeks.

Oden found that youngsters did best when paired with their own classmates. It seems likely that improvements in social skills were most readily maintained when they were observed by a girl or boy who was in regular daily contact with the target child.

On the other hand, when children had severe relationship problems, Oden found it best to have them do their first weeks of practice with age-mates who were not in their own classes. Once a skill level had been reached which would reasonably guarantee social acceptance, they turned to playing with classmates.

Oden reports that other researchers have combined the coaching procedure with behavior modification techniques which limit each play session to the practice of only one new skill and which enable the adult to slowly decrease his or her participation in the process. While this method takes longer, evaluations show that gains are maintained over a period of a year or more.

In another study, fourth and fifth graders who had difficulty in being flexible enough to compromise when playing with peers were trained to be more cooperative through behavior modification methods (Allen et al. 1975). Children were taught effective interpersonal skills and given opportunities to practice them during small-group games. Youngsters were reinforced for specific positive behaviors with tokens which they could exchange to purchase small toys and candies. Gains in social skill and in sociometric evaluation by peers persisted for at least a year after the experiment ended. The authors speculate that as youngsters became more successful at playing cooperatively, they began an upward spiral in their classmates' estimates of them as friends and in their ability to behave in socially acceptable ways.

Improved communication skills are also the goal of a number of ingenious games designed by McCaffrey in which players are trained to take other people's perspectives (Lavin 1977). These structured experiences involve colorful props and enjoyable tasks which make it fun for each player to find out enough about his or her partner to be able to communicate effectively.

Developing Assertiveness. Based on the observation that stressed youngsters are either withdrawn or overly aggressive, training programs have been devised to teach children to avoid both of these extremes and become pleasantly assertive. Bornstein, Bellack, and Hersen (1977) worked with eight- to eleven-year-olds who were withdrawn and thus isolated from their peers. They determined that their subjects needed to learn to make eye contact with others, to speak louder and longer, and to make more requests for help or for things they wanted. Working on these specific skills, youngsters were able to achieve considerable improvement in three weeks of brief training sessions.

Flowers and Booraem (1980) provided assertiveness training for fourth and fifth graders with equally promising results. Not only did their subjects become more assertive, but their grades, teacher ratings, and self-esteem improved. The specific training procedures they employed are described in detail in their book for parents and teachers, *Help Your Children Be Self Confident* (Booraem, Flowers, and Schwartz 1978).

Teaching Problem-Solving Skills. A great many of the efforts to help children learn to make friends have been directed at teaching problem-solving skills. As we have seen, youngsters who live in chronically stressful homes often have adult models who deal with all difficulties by using alcohol, drugs, or violence. In theory, if these children can be taught to think of many alternatives and to predict the consequences of each, they are more likely to be able to avoid the poor example set for them by their caretakers.

Researchers have shown that problem-solving ability can be taught to children as early as age four. Shure and Spivak (1979) find the technique especially helpful for youngsters who usually cope either by withdrawing or by impulsive acting out. They report that increased problem-solving ability has enabled inhibited youngsters to become more outgoing and better able to deal with confrontation. Impulsive children have become more patient and less angry. The authors find that youngsters can maintain their skill levels for two or more years without additional training.

Shure and Spivak describe impressive improvement in the coping skills of a group of inner-city four-year-olds who took part in one of their programs. In this instance, the preschoolers' mothers were taught how to train their own children to think of alternative solutions and to "foresee what might happen next if a solution is carried out" (Shure and Spivak 1979, 202).

While they were training their children, it is possible that these mothers improved their own problem-solving abilities and thus increased total family functioning. Practitioners may find that, when they can interest parents in implementing packaged training programs with their children, the adults may benefit as much as the youngsters.

Selman (undated) in his work with disturbed children at the Judge Baker Child Guidance Center in Boston, has designed a program which focuses specifically on interpersonal rather than general problem solving. Lavin (1977) describes the program's use in school settings with groups of children who have relationship problems. Fourth, fifth, and sixth graders first view a sound filmstrip which presents an interpersonal dilemma (e.g., what to do when a friend steals something, what to do when a youngster wants to make a new friend but doesn't want to hurt an old friend's feelings). The children then talk about the kinds of friendship issues they face in their own lives and together think of ways to solve the filmed dilemma and their own problems.

Teaching Children to Identify and Face Stress

Another major helping strategy involves teaching children to identify stressful situations and react to them in consciously planned ways. Youngsters need not rely solely on their own resources, responding unconsciously as best they can. Recently, practitioners have begun to develop programs to teach children about stress and about their own reactions to tension. The belief is that youngsters can learn how their bodies respond and how to control or change maladaptive reactions. These programs appear to be modeled on the stress reduction work being done with adult heart patients. Two examples of programs designed for use with children in the upper elementary grades illustrate the kinds of packages which are being marketed.

Programs to Identify and Reduce Stress

Schultz and Heuchert (1983) believe that school-age children can be taught to

  identify situations in school and home which are stressful

  predict when these events are likely to occur

  plan in advance for ways in which they will deal with the stress

  keep track of their successful and unsuccessful responses so that they can improve their ability to cope effectively

The authors describe a detailed training program which they have designed. Among its major elements are techniques for helping children to recognize psychologically stressful events. The children also learn how to check the accuracy of their perceptions with those of other participants. Youngsters are taught to record and evaluate their coping efforts so that they can clearly recognize and learn from their successes, as well as avoid repeating failures. Pupils learn to use their energy wisely, pacing themselves and resting periodically. They discover that problems can stay unsolved for a time while they catch their breath and relax. The authors predict that children who successfully complete the training program will develop a sense of power and mastery. Each new experience of consciously facing and experimenting with alternative ways of coping with stress will result in more self-confidence. However, no evaluative data are presented to support this prediction.

A similarly unproven but promising program for fourth through sixth grade children is outlined by Segal (1983). Pupils learn to identify stressors through a series of classroom presentations of tense situations. They then practice ways to deal with their feelings of anxiety. They are taught to look at stressful events from different points of view, to consciously relax their bodies, and to attack stress from a problem-solving stance. They also watch while others model appropriate coping strategies. In addition, youngsters are given instruction in assertiveness and in self-control.

A Proposed Helping Strategy

Most children are capable of understanding when something has gone awry in their lives and of identifying the cause when an adult helps them to do so. It is proposed that practitioners work with only one child at a time, designing unique programs for individuals. Under these circumstances, children as young as three years of age can be helped to accurately define the situation in their own terms, and to do something constructive that will make them feel better. As outlined in chapter 1, it is proposed that adults assist the coping process by helping the child eliminate at least one stressor in his or her life, by teaching new coping strategies, and by showing children how they can transfer existing techniques to other life situations.

Remove at Least One Stressor. As we have seen, combinations of stressors increase a child's coping difficulties in geometric rather than additive fashion (Rutter 1979). Thus, the cancellation of even one minor cause of stress can be helpful. The simple procedure of assisting youngsters to list all of the stresses they perceive in home and school environments can be expected to produce one or more candidates for removal. For example, when his mother's job loss forced them to move to a smaller apartment, Chris had to share a room with his retarded brother, Tim. This created a long list of tensions, and Chris' school performance began to decline. Chris identified one of the stresses as Tim's well-meaning but irritating habit of interrupting while Chris was trying to do his homework. With his mother's approval, Chris began going to the library to do his assignments. As a result, one source of stress was removed and Christopher's grades improved.

Teach New Coping Strategies. A careful examination of the individual's existing coping strategies will help the practitioner to decide which ones are effective and which have become self-destructive. Helping adults need to decide when

impulsive acting out is no longer a harmless anesthetic for the child's pain and has instead begun to get the youngster into serious trouble

denial, which at first helped maintain the child's equilibrium, now applies to feelings of pleasure as well as pain

regression, once a way to seek and receive needed comforting, now evokes annoyance from caretakers and teasing from peers

withdrawal is no longer a way of feeling safe in a dangerous situation, but is now a way of life which effectively blocks out help and warmth from others

When consequences are negative, children need to be taught more effective coping strategies. Each new technique will be most easily learned if it is close in style to the child's original unconscious choice. For example, Joshua's teacher helped him substitute sublimation for impulsive acting out as a coping technique after his mother deserted him. Josh's first impulse was to express his anger by running around the classroom, pushing furniture and people out of his way. His teacher helped him to think of several vigorous physical activities which would not be destructive but which would still serve to release his pent-up emotions. Depending on the time of day and the weather outside, they decided that Josh could stack books in the cupboard, run laps on the playground or in the gym, wash blackboards, or do push-ups in an unused classroom.

In some cases, of course, children have already faced the stress and chosen a coping strategy which has the potential for long-term effectiveness. Even so, they will need help if

altruism has changed from being a satisfying way of helping the family to being a burden that makes it impossible to be a child

suppression is no longer a way to temporarily set aside feelings of stress, but has turned into denial

anticipation, which once was a highly effective protective device, has become a compulsive fear of the unknown and the unexpected *sublimation,* instead of being a way to compensate for the negative events in life, is now an end in itself, with the child so engrossed that pleasure, pain, and the needs of others go unnoticed

humor has become biting wit turned savagely inward against the self when originally it was a way to relieve tension

When ordinarily effective coping strategies have gone sour, children need help to recognize what has happened and to modify their behavior. Again, the alterations they are asked to make work best when they are as near as possible to the original unconscious choice. For example, Sara's foster mother helped her to see that surprises can be fun and that Sara need not try to anticipate and control every area of her life. She began by having Sara help her to plan a successful surprise party for her foster father's birthday. This led to plans for other surprise visits and trips. Eventually Sara was willing to try a new experience that hadn't been planned in advance.

Transfer Coping Strategies to Other Life Situations. Rather than ask a child to abandon a coping strategy, it is often better to show the youngster how it can be used in a different area of life where it will be more productive. To do this, the child needs to be helped to evaluate the effectiveness of the various coping techniques he or she has been using and decide which can be transferred to other circumstances. For example, when her mother remarried, Nicole was overwhelmed by the adjustments she had to make to her new home and stepfather. She also was anxious about having to enter a new school at midsemester. In the three years after her father's death, Nicole had coped by becoming a role equal with her mother and she resented the idea of being demoted to the status of a child again. In talking about her feelings with a counselor, Nicky realized that she did not need to abandon her skills. She could use them to her advantage in becoming accepted in the new classroom. Nicole's well-developed ability to empathize and to be a sympathetic listener would certainly help her make friends with the children in the new school.

Effective Coping

There is as yet no definition of effective coping which permits an observer to rate a child's ability to handle stress. However, existing descriptions of good coping in adults may provide some tentative guidelines to help practitioners evaluate the progress made by their child clients. Descriptions of adult coping center around five areas of functioning: work achievement, use of leisure time, feelings, relationships, and sense of self.

Wortman's (1983) summary of a study of adult victims of violence finds that good copers are mentally healthy. They are able to express positive feelings. They are in reasonably good physical health. They function well in their daily work and leisure activities, and they believe that they have recovered from the stress they suffered as victims. Garmezy (1976), in studying adults whose childhoods had been chaotic, describes the good copers as people who work, play, love, and expect well. Vaillant (1979) equates good coping in adults with having a sense of contentment with self, being hopeful about life, being able to play and relax, being successful in work or career, and relating well to a mate.

Tentatively then, it seems reasonable to base judgments of effective coping in children on evaluations of their ability to maintain reasonable achievement standards in school, enjoy play, express their emotions, believe in their own competence and worth, and relate well to others. Of course, even good copers will be more able in some areas and less so in others.

School

As we have seen, children's schoolwork almost always suffers when their lives become stressful. Youngsters who cope effectively, gradually make up previous academic losses and return to their normal achievement levels. They may still require one-to-one help from teachers for some time before they can begin to work independently. At the opposite extreme, youngsters whose school performance while under stress was "too good to be true," give evidence of their effective adaptation by being able to maintain their standards, yet show less compulsiveness about getting top grades.

Play

Children who cope effectively with stress are able to enjoy play. They become involved. They smile and laugh, and their bodies are relaxed. They use play to symbolically reenact their problems, solving them and overcoming imagined aggressors. In comparison, Terr (1981) finds that children who are anxious and unable to cope are also unable to use play to relieve tension. Instead, they repeat traumatic incidents in literal ways that are sometimes frightening rather than soothing.

Feelings

Good copers are aware of their feelings and can label and express them. They know and use constructive techniques to vent negative emotions. They express caring for others and accept that they are worthy of being loved. Some are able to use objects (blankets, stuffed animals) or to recall songs, poems, books, or incidents which symbolize the love they share with a caretaker. These help them feel cherished when alone or in a strange place and serve as sources of solace in times of stress (Horton 1981).

Sense of Self

Children who cope effectively have had the experience of successfully facing and conquering stress. They have a sense of being competent. They see themselves as worthwhile and valuable people. They are optimistic about their ability to survive whatever life brings.

Relationships

The ability to make and keep friends provides a cushion of support for children who cope effectively. They have role models and people to turn to outside of their families who are sources of cheer and encouragement. They have learned to trust and to be trustworthy. They have opened themselves to intimacy.

References

Allen, R.P., D.J. Safer, R. Heaton, A. Ward, and M. Barrell. 1975. Behavior therapy for socially ineffective chldren. *Journal of the American Academy of Child Psychiatry,* 14:500–509.

Booraem, C.D., J.V. Flowers, and B. Schwartz. 1978. *Help your children be self confident.* Englewood Cliffs, N..J.: Prentice-Hall.

Bornstein, M.R., A.S. Bellack, and M. Hersen. 1977. Social-skills training for unassertive children: A multiple-baseline analysis. *Journal of Applied Behavior Analysis,* 10:183–195.

Bronfenbrenner, U. 1976. The disturbing changes in the American family. *Search* (State University of New York), 2:4–10.

Cartledge, G., and J.F. Milburn. 1980. *Teaching social skills to children.* New York: Pergamon Press.

Chandler, L.A. 1982. *Children under stress: Understanding emotional adjustment reactions.* Springfield, Ill.: Charles C. Thomas Publisher.

Flowers, J.V., and C.D. Booraem. 1980. Simulation and role playing methods. In *Helping people change: A textbook of methods,* second edition, ed. F.H. Kanfer, and A.P. Goldstein. New York: Pergamon Press.

Garmezy, N. 1976. *Vulnerable and invulnerable children: Theory, research and intervention.* Master lecture on developmental psychology, no. 1337. Washington, D.C.: American Psychological Association.

Horton, P.C. 1981. *Solace: The missing dimension in psychiatry*. Chicago: The University of Chicago Press.

Lavin, D.R. 1977. Developmental interventions to stimulate social awareness and communication skills. Expanded version of a paper presented at the annual conference of the American Orthopsychiatric Association, New York. Mimeo.

Oden, S. 1982. The applicability of social skills training research. Department of Advanced Study in Early Childhood Education, Wheelock College. Mimeo.

Rubin, Z. 1980. *Children's friendships*. The Developing Child Series. Cambridge: Harvard University Press.

Rutter, M. 1979. Protective factors in children's responses to stress and disadvantage. In *Primary prevention of psychopathology, Volume III, Social competence in children*, ed. M.W. Kent and J.E. Rolf. Hanover, N.H.: University Press of New England.

————. 1983. Stress, coping, and development: Some issues and some questions. In *Stress, coping and development in children*, ed. N. Garmezy and M. Rutter. New York: McGraw-Hill Book Company.

Schultz, E.W., and C.M. Heuchert. 1983. *Child stress and the school experience*. New York: Human Sciences Press, Inc.

Segal, J. 1983. Utilization of stress and coping research: Issues of public education and public policy. In *Stress, coping, and development in children*, ed. N. Garmezy and M. Rutter. New York: McGraw-Hill Book Company.

Selman, R.L. undated. *Relationships and values*. New York: Guidance Associates. Sound Filmstrip Program.

Selman, R.L., and A.P. Selman. 1979. Children's ideas about friendship: A new theory. *Psychology Today*, October.

Shure, M.B., and G. Spivak, 1979. Interpersonal problem solving thinking and adjustment in the mother-child dyad. In *Primary prevention of psychopathology, Volume III, Social competence in children*, ed. M.W. Kent and J.E. Rolf. Hanover, N.H.: University Press of New England.

Stocking, S.H., D. Arezzo, and S. Leavitt. 1980. *Helping kids make friends*. Niles, Ill.: Argus Communications.

Terr, L.C. 1981. "Forbidden games": Post-traumatic child's play. *Journal of the American Academy of Child Psychiatry*, 20:741–760.

Vaillant, G.E. 1977. *Adaptation to life*. Boston: Little, Brown and Company.

Werner, E.E., and R.S. Smith. 1982. *Vulnerable but invincible: A longitudinal study of resilient children and youth*. New York: McGraw-Hill Book Company.

Wortman, C.B. 1983. Coping with victimization: Conclusions and implications for future research. *Journal of Social Issues*, 39:195–221.

Index

About the Author

Avis Brenner invented and nurtured a unique program at Lesley College which trains women to work effectively with children under stress. She developed the project in cooperation with more than one hundred human service agencies in the Boston area, encouraging innovative professionals to come to the campus to present their research on childhood stress. Dr. Brenner received her Ed.D. in social psychology from Columbia University in 1968, her M.A. from Ohio State University in 1950, and her A.B. from Antioch College in 1947. She has been a fashion magazine editor and writer specializing in the problems of working women, an elementary school teacher, and a professor of education at Hunter College and Lesley College. In 1983 she embarked on a new career as a consultant, writer, and sculptor. Her works in bronze are figurative studies of joyous and stressful interactions among children and adults.